Emma Elizabeth Page

Heart culture

A text book for teaching kindness to animals

Emma Elizabeth Page

Heart culture
A text book for teaching kindness to animals

ISBN/EAN: 9783337149758

Printed in Europe, USA, Canada, Australia, Japan

Cover: Foto ©Lupo / pixelio.de

More available books at **www.hansebooks.com**

HEART CULTURE.

A Text Book for Teaching Kindness to Animals,
Arranged for Use in Public and
Private Schools

BY
EMMA E. PAGE
Organizer and Lecturer for the National Department of Mercy.

SAN FRANCISCO
THE WHITAKER & RAY CO.
(INCORPORATED)
1897

Dedication.

> "Go little booke, God send thee good passage,
> And specially, let this be thy prayre
> Unto them all that thee shall read or hear,
> Where thou art wrong, after their help to call,
> Thee to correct in any part or all."
> —*Chaucer.*

HEART CULTURE is dedicated to the home circle, father, mother, sisters, brothers, who have filled my hands with good seed and untiringly stayed my steps while I planted the gift. If from this planting, one flower of truth or joy or mercy bloom in any heart, its beauty and its fragrance all are theirs by right.

PREFACE.

"**My People are destroyed for lack of Knowledge.**"

The aim of this book is to teach kindness to animals by quickening sympathy for them, arousing a sense of justice toward them, and instilling the fundamental principles of right care of them.

I have not attempted scientific nature study, but I have earnestly striven to avoid being unscientific, which is, perhaps, more difficult.

How to care for domestic animals is dwelt upon with considerable detail, because these things must be taught in school to get down into the family life of all the people. Not to know is often as cruel as not to care.

I have avoided remarkable anecdotes, feeling that the desired end would be better served by common experiences of barnyard and field.

If Bands of Mercy are formed according to the suggestion in the back of the book, the school may be given practical moral activity, which is of the utmost importance.

George T. Angell gives the very best argument for this kind of teaching.

"I am sometimes asked, 'Why do you spend so much of your time and money in talking about kindness to animals, when there is so much cruelty to men?' And I answer, 'I am working at the roots.' Every humane publication, every lecture, every step, in doing or teaching kindness to animals is a step to prevent crime, a step in promoting the growth of those qualities of heart which will elevate human souls, even in the dens of sin and shame, and prepare the way for the coming of peace on earth and good will to men."

The unmistakable moral uplift given to pupils in English and French schools where this kind of teaching has passed beyond the line of experiment into accepted practice, justifies Mr. Angell's faith.

While covering the definite ground of mercy to animals I have earnestly sought to make it a work of character building for the pupils.

The motto of each chapter is a sort of truth-rule to measure action by, and may be made as distinctly helpful as rules of arithmetic and grammar. The teacher should put the lesson motto on the board each week and have it thoroughly committed, and the various mottoes with the leading principles should be reviewed from time to time as in other branches.

An extended list of questions is appended to each chapter to aid the teacher in bringing out discussion of the important points. It is hoped that immediate needs of time and place will receive special attention.

Encourage the pupils of every grade to careful observation of all life about them. Have them present written studies on the animals that interest them most and in all practical ways stimulate them to acurate observation of the characteristics and habits of Mother Nature's children. This will develop hand and head and heart, the inseparable three fold humanity. A few years ago the cry from thoughtful educators was: "Add physical culture to our curriculum and all will be well. This has been done to the great help of many schools. But the growing number of educated criminals proves that something still is lacking. Heart Culture is now the watchword, passed along the line and when it shall take its rightful place with the culture of mind and body, the child character will round out into nobler manhood and womanhood. Since good citizenship is the object of the public school, that is preeminently the place for this triune teaching. A single chapter in this book may furnish material for several lessons, especially those in Parts Third and Fourth.

Sarah J. Eddy, (who should wear the title of "Good"), George T. Angell, founder of the American Band of Mercy, Mary F. Lovell, National Mercy Superintendent, Lydia A. Irons, Assistant National Mercy Superintendent, Mrs. H. Marie Currey, Superintendent of Hygienic Cookery for Western Washington, and Sara Thomas, Mercy Superintendent of Arkansas, are some of the wise good friends who have my warm thanks go out to them and many others who have lent a hand. If teachers and pupils find in the book helps to justice and mercy, truth, and honor in the schoolroom, on the playground, at home and in the fields, that will be a rich reward to them and to me.

CONTENTS.

PART FIRST.

	PAGE.
CHAPTER I—Muff's Lesson	9
CHAPTER II—Scatter Seeds of Kindness	12
CHAPTER III—Three Little Chickens	15
CHAPTER IV—"The Happy Meadows."	18
CHAPTER V—Wishing	23
CHAPTER VI—Three Little Bugs in a Basket	26
CHAPTER VII—The Birdies' Lullaby	29
CHAPTER VIII—Three Little Nest-Birds	31
CHAPTER IX—The Butterfly Fad	36
CHAPTER X—The Mother Rabbit	40
CHAPTER XI—The Humming Bird's Wedding	42
CHAPTER XII—The Small Life of Sea and Shore	46
CHAPTER XIII—Kindness Makes Paradise	52

PART SECOND.

CHAPTER XIV—What Strength is For	59
CHAPTER XV—True Courage	63
CHAPTER XVI—The Bluebird and the Sparrow	67
CHAPTER XVII—The Law of Habit	72
CHAPTER XVIII—Honesty	76
CHAPTER XIX—Dovetrot's Way	80
CHAPTER XX—Traps	84
CHAPTER XXI—Fish and Harmless Reptiles	89
CHAPTER XXII—Pets	95
CHAPTER XXIII—Friends of School and Home	100
CHAPTER XXIV—A Caged Lark	108

PART THIRD.

CHAPTER XXV—Cats 115
CHAPTER XXVI—The Dog 121
CHAPTER XXVII—The Dog—(Continued) 127
CHAPTER XXVIII—Sheep 134
CHAPTER XXIX—Sheep—(Continued) 140
CHAPTER XXX—The Hog 144
CHAPTER XXXI—The Cow 149
CHAPTER XXXII—The Care of the Cow 153
CHAPTER XXXIII—The Horse 160
CHAPTER XXXIV—The Care of the Horse 169
CHAPTER XXXV—The Mule and the Burro 179
CHAPTER XXXVI—The Common Hen 185
CHAPTER XXXVII—Domestic Water Fowls 193
CHAPTER XXXVIII—Turkeys, Guineas and Pea Fowls 201
CHAPTER XXXIX—Pigeons, Parrots and Song Birds. 209

PART FOURTH.

CHAPTER XL—Birds and Agriculture 219
CHAPTER XLI—Cost of Feather Ornaments 228
CHAPTER XLII—Hunting 237
CHAPTER XLIII—Field Glass and Microscope 247
CHAPTER XLIV—Peace and Arbitration 255
"The Voice of the Dove" 261
"The Thrush's Lesson" 262
"To My Dog Blanco" 263
"The Legend of the Coyote" 264
Subjects for Essays 267
How to Form a Band of Mercy 268
"One Band of Mercy in San Francisco" 269
How to Kill Humanely 272

PART FIRST.

In which a special effort is made to teach that kindness or goodness is in "Doing," to quicken sympathetic observation of all life close about the little ones, and to develop an affectionate regard for each and all in their rightful place.

CHAPTER I.
MUFF'S LESSON.

"To be Good is to do Good."

One of Ruth's Christmas presents was a beautiful white kitty. Its soft white fur and pretty pink mouth made her think of her warm white muff with its pink silk linings, so she named the kitty Muff.

She was anxious that Muff should have good manners and morals, so one morning, when kitty was at breakfast, the little mistress gave her a long lesson. Her text was this: "To be good is to do good." And she explained what it meant with great care. Listen closely and see if you can tell over all the points when the lesson is ended. I am sure you can, because you are older than you were yesterday and can do more.

"TO BE GOOD IS TO DO GOOD."

Come learn your lesson, kitty Muff.
　Now listen! Look right here!
To be good is to do good, Muff;
　You understand, my dear?

That means, don't fret your mother, Muff,
　And never spill your milk;
Be sure and wash yourself all clean,
　And keep your fur like silk.

Speak gently when you're worried, Muff,
　That's where the good depends;
For kindness makes a music-voice,
　That wins you lots of friends.

Don't scratch nor bite! No! Not in fun!
　And never strike! That's rough;
And never, never catch a bird!
　No, not if hungry, Muff.

It's mean to hurt the smallest thing,
　Hard-hearted folks do so;
To be hard-hearted is the worst
　Of anything I know.

"To be good is to do good," Muff,
　As good as good can be;
That means, "If I'll be nice to you,
　That you'll be nice to me."
　　　　　　　　　　Emma E. Page.

　This is a long lesson, but Muff seems to take it all in as you see by the picture. If a kitty could learn so much, I

am sure our boys and girls can do more—they can tell it.
Now, tell me as fast as you can how many different things
Ruth told Muff to do, and not to do.

First she calls for close attention, and then she gives
twelve points. If you have given close attention, you can
tell over all these points.

QUESTIONS.

If it is good manners for a kitty not to fret its mother,
what of boys and girls?

If a kitty should be neat about her eating, what of you?

Let the teacher follow out this same line of questions,
encouraging free expression among the children. Bring
out the points made to Muff on scratching, biting, striking, washing, combing, bird catching, and make the
school understand that—

If these are good lessons for a kitty, how much more
important they are for children.

If it is mean for a kitty to hurt any little creature, how
much worse is it for children?

What kind of people hurt birds and dogs and kitties?

What does Ruth say is the worst thing she knows?

What does she say will help the kitty to be good to her?

Commit the last four lines.

Would it help work and play if boys and girls would try
this with each other? Mary can't control Johnny's voice,
but she can control her own. She can't control Johnny's
hand, but she can control her own, so if she makes her
voice gentle in times of trouble and her hand helpful in
times of hurry, she will make it easier for him to do the
same, and they and every one about them will be happier.

CHAPTER II.

"Scatter Seeds of Kindness."

" To be good is to do good," Muff,
As good as good can be!
That means, " If I'll be nice to you,
That you'll be nice to me."

This part of Muff's lesson is the very best rule for a happy life. It is not only the rule for brothers and sisters and for schoolmates, but may be carried out with pets and their owners. The boy that does not make his dog or his horse happier for being with him, has not learned the first secret of right ownership. And the girl whose bird does not sing sweeter at her coming, and whose cat does not purr louder at her touch, ought not to have them.

The child that grows up neglectful of pets, or unkind to them may become unkind to father and mother, brother and sister.

Kind words and kind acts are like seeds planted in the garden of the heart, they grow and make more and more kind words and deeds, perhaps fairer and sweeter than the old.

A sweet pea seed was dropped under a window, and it sprouted and grew till it reached the window sill and spread itself out in a bank of green.

By and by when the days were long and the nights were warm, it sent out hundreds of blossoms like pink-winged banners that waved in the soft wind and sent a sweet breath through the garden and house. Everybody said: "How lovely the sweet peas are!" A smile, a pleasant word, a gentle act are seeds of kindness that may grow and blossom even sweeter than the pea.

Then scatter seeds of kindness and the school room will be like a garden of sweet peas, the playground will be bright with sunshine and the home will be full of "music-

voices." "Then scatter seeds of kindness" that they may grow and grow and fill the house and the garden, the school and the town with their beauty.

QUESTIONS.

What is the motto of this lesson?
Commit the four lines from Muff's lesson?
What is the secret of a happy life?
To how many different people does this apply?
Does it apply to pets?
How should a boy's horse feel toward him?
How should a girl's bird feel when she comes near it?

How does a kitty show her pleasure in being petted?

If we are always good and gentle, are our pets likely to be gentle too and enjoy being with us?

What is kindness like?

Seeds grow in the ground, where does kindness grow?

If a seed grows does it make just one more seed or many?

If kindness is put in people's hearts and given a chance, will it grow and make more?

(Get the children to give instances of kindness begetting kindness that they have seen and known.)

Tell about the sweet pea.

How many blossoms did it have?

How tall did the pea vine grow?

How far did its perfume reach?

May kindness spread like the perfume?

What are the seeds of kindness?

If the boys and girls would scatter them thick and fast, how would the schoolroom be?

How would the playground be?

How would our home be?

What does kindness do to the voice?

What does it do to the face?

What does it do for the hands and feet?

CHAPTER III.
THREE LITTLE CHICKS.
"Let's share the Treat."

(Let these verses be given with the action the words suggest. Let the voices imitate the call of the chick in "Terwhit! Terwheet!" Have the school give it us a concert exercise.)

    Three little chicks, so downy and neat,
    Went out in search of something to eat.
"Terwhit! Terwheet! Something to eat!"
    And soon they picked up a straw of wheat.

Said one little chick: "This belongs to me."
Said the other little chick: "We'll see! We'll see!"
"Terwhit! Terwheet! It's nice and sweet!"
Said number three: "Let's share the treat."

Then one chick seized the straw in his bill,
And was just preparing to eat his fill,
When the other little chick stepped up so quick,
He hadn't a chance for a picnic pick.

They pulled and they tugged, the downy things,
And Oh, how they flapped their baby wings!
"Terwhit! Terwheet! It's mine to eat.
Just please let go this bit of wheat."

And fiercer and fiercer the battle grew,
Until the straw broke right in two,
And the little chicks were in a fix,
And sorry enough for their naughty tricks.

For a saucy crow had watched their flight,
And he laughs: "Ha ha! It serves you right!"
Then he snatched the prize before their eyes,
And over the hills and away—he flies.

From Olive Plants.

Notice that the chickies seemed to all find the straw together and one wanted to take it all himself. But even if one had found it alone, would it not have been nice of him to have shared it with the others? They were all of one family. The selfishness of the two led them into a quarrel and the quarrel made them lose the prize. Because the crow was big and strong and selfish, he snatched it all away from them. Selfishness is always bad. "Let's share the treat." Let's give our friends and playmates part of the good things. "Let's share the treat."

QUESTIONS.

What is the motto of this lesson?
Which chick gave the motto?
What did the two selfish ones do?
What happened to them?
What happened to the straw of wheat?
Why did the crow take it?
If chicks or children let a selfish spirit rule them, is it likely to grow bigger as they grow bigger?
Was the third little chick hungry?
Did it have a right to a share?
What is fair and kind to do with any good thing?
Repeat the motto in concert.

CHAPTER IV.

"THE HAPPY MEADOW."

*"Beautiful life of earth and air,
Beautiful creatures everywhere."*

"I will try to be kind to all living creatures and protect them from cruel usage."

OVER IN THE MEADOW—MRS. OLIVE A. WADSWORTH.

[*From the Humane Educator.*]

(The action of this piece can be arranged at will, but it does best if each child who has recited imitates the action of the others, so that by degrees all join in it. This is particularly adapted for a group of boys.)

FIRST BOY—
Over in the meadow, in the sand, in the sun,
Lived an old mother toad and her little toady one,
"Wink!" said the mother; "I wink," said the one;
So she winked and she blinked, in the sand, in the sun.

SECOND BOY—
Over in the meadow, where the stream runs blue,
Lived an old mother fish, and her little fishes two.
"Swim!" said the mother; "We swim," said the two;
So they swam and they leaped where the stream runs blue.

THIRD BOY—
Over in the meadow, in a hole in the tree,
Lived a mother bluebird, and her little birdies three.

"Sing!" said the mother; "We sing," said the three;
So they sang and were glad in the hole in the tree.

FOURTH BOY—
Over in the meadow, in the reeds on the shore,
Lived a mother musk-rat and her little ratties four.
"Dive!" said the mother; "We dive," said the four;
So they dived and they burrowed in the reeds on the shore.

FIFTH BOY—
Over in the meadow, in the snug beehive,
Lived a mother honey bee and her little honeys five.
"Buzz!" said the mother; "We buzz," said the five;
So they buzzed and they hummed in the snug beehive.

SIXTH BOY—
Over in the meadow, by the old mossy gate,
Lived a brown mother lizard and her little lizards eight.
"Bask!" said the mother; "We bask," said the eight;
So they basked in the sun on the old mossy gate.

SEVENTH BOY—
Over in the meadow, where the clear pools shine,
Lived a green mother frog and her little froggies nine.
"Croak!" said the mother; "We croak," said the nine;
So they croaked and they splashed where the clear pools shine.

EIGHTH BOY—
Over in a meadow, in a sly little den,
Lived a gray mother spider and her little spiders ten.
"Spin!" said the mother; "We spin," said the ten;
So they spun lace webs in their sly little den.

NINTH BOY—
Over in the meadow, where the men dig and delve,
Lived a wise mother ant and her little anties twelve.
"Toil!" said the mother; "We toil," said the twelve;
So they toiled and were wise where the men dig and delve.

This was a happy meadow with so many beautiful, happy creatures in it. If you can't find all of these in every meadow, you are sure to find some of them if you look closely. Be sure you look with your eyes and not with your hands. Some children think they must see all such things with their hands, but that is a great mistake. Not a single one of these creatures mentioned in this happy meadow would like to be touched, and you would not bring distress into the happy meadow and spoil its name, would you?

Toads are very useful, therefore very happy; they are the best kind of fly traps. In Paris and other places they are kept in gardens to clear the plants of insects. So they are one of our helpers and never hurt any one. Take good care of them then, whether you meet them in the happy meadow or some place else.

How beautiful the fish are in the streams! They help to keep the water clean and pure. See! They are helpers, too. Don't take them from their home and put them in globes and jars. They lose their chance to help, lose most of their beauty and lose their happy spirit. Don't think it play to catch the little minnows. They are so beautiful and so happy where the stream runs blue.

Bluebirds are our friends, for they eat up the insects that would spoil our apples and plums. They want us to be very respectful though, and keep hands off of them and their nests. So let us be very careful not to offend them. You can watch the blue wings fan the air. You can hear the short sweet song; but don't lay a finger on the nest, for the bird would leave it and build another. That would be robbing it of all its hard work, and spoiling its first happy home.

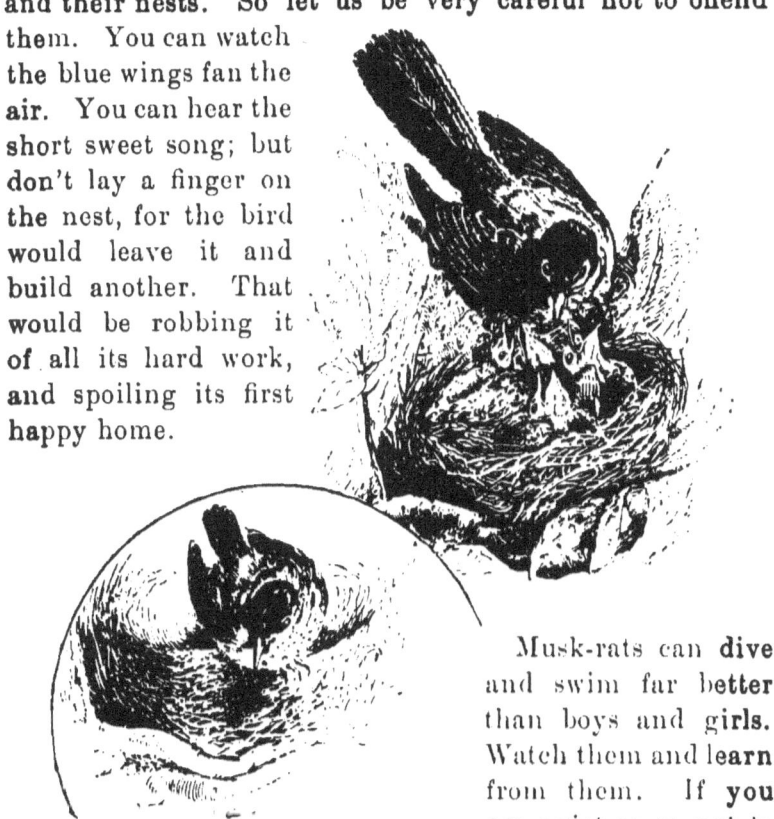

Musk-rats can **dive and swim far better than boys and girls. Watch them and learn from them. If you are quiet so as not to** disturb or frighten them, they will show you many a cute trick. If you are very gentle in your movements, you can get quite near.

" O velvet bee, you're a dusty fellow!
You've powdered your legs with gold."

How nice the honey is he makes for us! Even the bees that only make honey for themselves, help to make good things grow for us. They carry the pollen from flower to flower, so as to make more seeds and fruits. The bees are wonderful workers and helpers. Take good care of every one.

Lizards like the warm sun and so you may often see them. Many have beautiful colors. Think how much you like the sun after it has been cold and cloudy. And then remember that lizards like it even better than you do and don't disturb them. These common little lizards never harm any one, so it would be cruel to harm them.

How happy the frogs are about a pool and how they can leap! Like the fish, they help to keep the water clean, and like toads they help to eat up troublesome insects. They are double helpers. If you should see any one throw a stick or a stone at a frog, tell him this and surely no fair person would go on abusing a little creature that does no wrong, and so merrily does all the good he can.

Spiders catch flies, too, in their silken web of lace.

The busy little ant is so wise and so happy about her work. Don't touch, but watch her, and you will learn many wonderful things.

No wonder that was a happy meadow, for all were helpers there. Helpers make happiness anywhere and happiness makes beauty.

> Beautiful life of earth and air!
> Beautiful helpers everywhere!

Take care of all these things and you will be helpers in this world of use and beauty.

CHAPTER V.
WISHING.

" There's nothing so Kingly as Kindness,
There's nothing so Royal as Truth."

" I wish I were *Queen!* " little Mabel cried,
 " I know what I'd do with the treasure!
I'd scatter it wide on every side,
 For everybody's pleasure.
Then would children at play and the lambs on the green,
And the birds and the bees laugh because I was Queen."
" You are Queen of your *life*," sang the little brown thrush,
 " With a *heart full* of *love's* golden treasure;
O, scatter it wide on every side,
 For *everybody's* pleasure.
Then will children at play, and the lambs on the green,
And the birds and the bees, laugh because *you* are *Queen.*"
" I wish I were *King*," little Henry cried,
 " I know what *I'd* do with the treasure!
I'd shower it down over country and town,
 For everybody's pleasure.
Then songs of rejoicing would make the earth ring,
Hard times would be over, because I was King."
" You are King of your *life*," sang the gay bobolink,
 " With *millions of heart*-gold for treasure;
O, shower it down over country and town,
 For *everybody's pleasure.*
Then songs of rejoicing will make the earth ring,
Hard times will be over, because *you* are *King.*"

Emma E. Page.

Questions.

What is the motto of this lesson?
What does "kingly" mean?
Why is kindness kingly?
What does "royal" mean?
What did Mabel wish for?
Why did she want to be Queen?
What did she think she would do with so much treasure?
What did she think the children, and the lambs, and the birds, and the bees, would do if she were Queen?
Why would they laugh?
What did the thrush tell her?
What is Love's golden treasure?
If you give out kindness, does your supply run out?
Can money do as much as kindness can, toward making people happy?
What does the thrush say will happen if she gives out her kindness on every side?
What did Henry wish to be?
Do we have a King in this country?
Did Henry want to be King, for just the same reason that Mabel did?
Did you ever hear a boy or girl wish to be rich?
What did Henry say about hard times?
Did any of you ever hear of hard times?
Do you know that selfishness and cruelty make the hardest of all hard times?
Do you know that boys and girls can make hard times for the dogs, and cats, and cows, and horses about them?

Do you know that they can make hard times for each other?
What did the bobolink tell Henry?
Is " heart-gold " the same as " love's golden treasure? "
What did he say would happen if Henry would shower it down over country and town?
Were the thrush and the bobolink agreed?
Do you think they were right?
Can we have plenty of heart-gold, if we will?
Can we have all the money we want?
Is it wise to make the most of the things we have?
Repeat the motto again in concert.

CHAPTER VI.
THREE LITTLE BUGS IN A BASKET.
Love makes Room.

Three little bugs in a basket,
  And hardly room for two;
One was yellow and one was black,
  And one like me and you.
The place was small no doubt for all,
  And what should three bugs do?

Three little bugs in a basket,
  And hardly crumbs for two;
And all were selfish in their hearts,
  The same as me or you.
The strong ones said, "We'll eat the bread!
  And that is what we'll do!"

Three little bugs in a basket,
  And the bed but two would hold;
So all three fell to quarreling,
  The white, the black and the gold.
And two of the bugs got under the rugs,
  And one was left in the cold.

Then he that was left in the basket,
  Without a crumb to chew,
Or a thread to wrap himself withal,
  When the wind across him blew,
Pulled one of the rugs from one of the bugs,
  And so the quarrel grew.

And then there was war in the basket!
    Ah, pity 'tis 'tis true!
    And he that was left to freeze and
        starve,
    A strength from his weakness
        drew.
    And he pulled the rugs from both
        of the bugs,
    And killed and ate them—too.

Now, when bugs live in a basket,
    Though more than it well can hold,

It seems to me they would better agree,
The white, the black, and the gold,
And share what comes of bed and crumbs,
And leave no bug in the cold.
     From "Voice Education."

QUESTIONS.

What is the motto of this lesson?
First, what did the bugs *seem* to lack?
Second, what did they seem to lack?
Third, what did they seem to lack?
While they seem to lack room, and bread, and crumbs, what they *really lacked* was love for each other.
What did the strong bugs do?
What should they have done?
What did the bug that was left to freeze and starve do, at last?
Then what happened in the basket?
How *might* they have lived in the basket?
What might love have done for them?
Repeat the motto in concert.

CHAPTER VII.

THE BIRDIES' LULLABY.

"Beautiful hands are those that do
Things that are kind and brave and true."

A bird sang softly on her nest,
 "Lullaby! Lullaby!"
To hush the wee ones 'neath her breast,
 "Lullaby!"

"Be still, my own, and sweetly sleep,
 Lullaby! Lullaby!
While I a mother's watch will keep,
 Lullaby!"

"My wings shall hide you from the dew,
 Lullaby! Lullaby!
And from the cold the whole night through,
 Lullaby!"

" Then sleep and rest, nor dream of fear,
    Lullaby! Lullaby!
What harm can chance while mother's near,
    Lullaby!"

" And when the rosy morn shall break,
    Lullaby! Lullaby!
I'll sing my birdlings wide awake,
    Lullaby!"

Emma E. Page.

QUESTIONS.

What is the motto of this lesson?
Did the mother bird do the things that are kind and brave and true?
In the second verse what did she promise the little birds?
In the third verse what two things did she promise?
Will she guard her little ones from harm all the night?
What will she do when morning comes?
Do your mothers do as much and more for you?
Would you do so much for them?
Would you do so much for brothers and sisters and playmates?
Would you like to have beautiful hands?
Can you make them beautiful with kindly deeds?
Repeat the motto again in concert.

CHAPTER VIII.
THREE LITTLE NEST-BIRDS.
JULIANA HORATIA EWING.
[*From Humane Educator.*]

"There are some Wrong Things we can Never Undo."

This poem is very attractive if recited by one little girl, with a boy and girl on each side of her, to imitate her actions in dumb show, and the following directions are carried out: We have taken the pledge—fold hands, point to Susan, Jimmy and I (point to self) each time the names are spoken. Up to sky—all point upwards. Shouted for glee—clap hands. Told us to put them back—raised finger. Crying alack—pretend to weep. Each took one— each child point one. Oh, dear! Oh, dear!—all hang heads and wring hands. Terrible thing to have heart-ache— hands of all to hearts. Mother said—all shake heads slowly. The bitterest tears—hands to eyes. Have buried— all point to the ground. Leaves that the branches— imitate falling leaves with both hands and fingers. And let all six arms drop to the sides limply, and heads hang at the words "are dead."

  We meant to be very kind;
   But if we ever find
Another soft, gray-green, moss-coated, feather-lined nest
  in a hedge,
  We have taken a pledge—
Susan, Jimmy and I—with remorseful tears, at this very
  minute,

That if there are eggs or little birds in it,
Robin, or wren, thrush, chaffinch, or linnet,
    We'll leave them there
    To their mother's care.

There were three of us—Kate, Susan and Jim—
    And three of them;
I don't know their names, for they couldn't speak
Except a little bit of a squeak
    Exactly like Poll—
    Susan's squealing doll.
  But squeaking dolls will lie on the shelves
  For years, and never squeak of themselves;
The reason we like little birds so much better than toys,
Is because they are really alive and know how to make a noise.

There were three of us, and three of them;
Kate—that is I, Susan and Jim,
    Our mother was busy making a pie,
    And theirs we think was up in the sky;
But for all Susan, Jimmy, or I can tell,
She may have been getting their dinner as well.
    They were left to themselves (and so were we)
    In a nest in the hedge by the willow-tree,
And when we caught sight of three red little fluff-tufted,
hazel-eyed, open-mouthed, pink-throated heads, we all shouted for glee.

    The way we really did wrong was this:
      We took them in for mother to kiss,
      And she told us to put them back;

While on the weeping-willow their mother was crying
"Alack!"
We really heard
Both what mother told us to do and the voice of the mother-bird.

But we three—that is, Susan and I, and Jim—
Thought we knew better than either of them;
And in spite of our mother's command and the poor bird's cry,
We determined to bring up the three little nestling ourselves on the sly.
We each took one,
It did seem such excellent fun!
Susan fed hers on milk and bread;
Jim got wriggling worms for his instead.
I gave mine meat,
For, you know, I thought, "Poor darling pet! why shouldn't it have roast beef to eat?"
But oh, dear! oh, dear! How we cried
When in spite of milk and bread and worms, and roast beef, the little birds died!

It's a terrible thing to have heart-ache.
I thought mine would break
As I heard the mother-bird's moan,
And looked at the gray-green, moss-coated, feather-lined nest she had taken such pains to make,
And her three little children dead and cold as a stone.
Mother said, and its sadly true:
"There are some wrong things one can never undo."
And nothing we could do or say
Would bring life back to the birds that day.

The bitterest tears that we could weep
Wouldn't wake them out of their stiff, cold sleep.
    But then,
We—Susan and Jim and I—mean never to be so selfish and wilful and cruel again.
And we three have buried that other three
In a soft, green moss-covered, flower-lined grave at the foot of the willow tree.
And all the leaves which its branches shed
We think are tears, because they are dead.

QUESTIONS.

What pledge did the three children take?
Do you think it is a good pledge?
Why did they like the birds so much better than toys?
What was the children's mother doing?
What do you think the little birdies' mother was doing?
Where were the young birds?
What did they look like?
Describe the nest?
Why did the children take the birdies out in the first place?
What did their mother tell them to do?
What did the mother bird want them to do?
What did the children think about it?
What did they decide to do?
What did they feed the birds?
Did they thrive?
How did the children feel about the loss of the birds?
How did the mother bird feel?

What did the children's mother say?
Did the children's sorrow undo the wrong?
Could anything undo it?
Is it right to grieve and distress others for our own pleasure?
Was it selfish of the children to take the birds?
What else was it besides selfish?
Where did they bury the birds?
In what kind of a grave?

CHAPTER IX.
THE BUTTERFLY FAD.

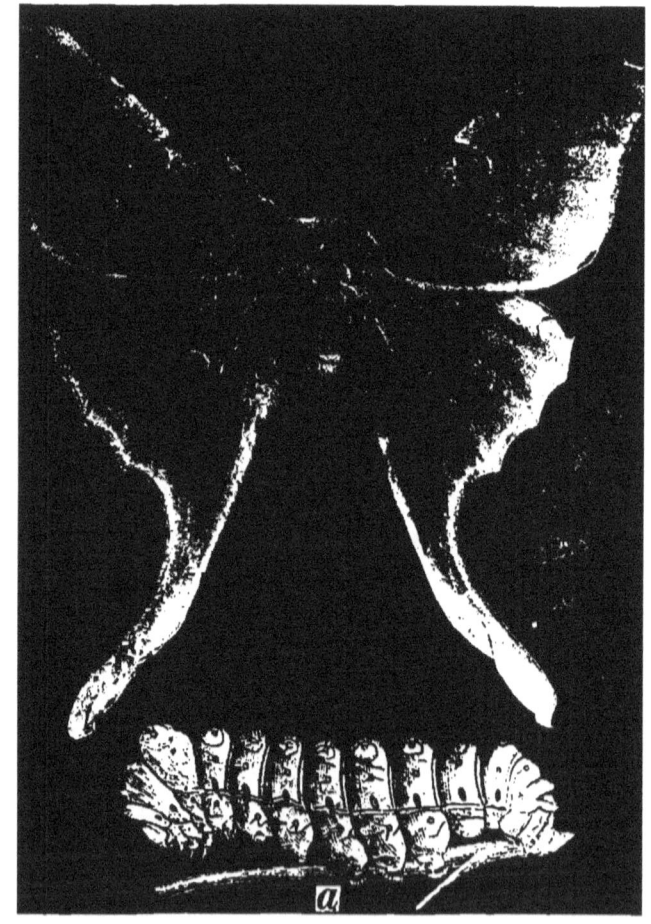

ELLA WHEELER WILCOX.

"O, wad some power the gifty gie us
To see ourselves as ithers see us!"

I happened one night in my travels
    To stray into Butterfly Vale,
Where my wondering eyes beheld butterflies
    With wing that were wide as a sail.
They lived in such houses of grandeur,
    Their days were successions of joys,
And the very last fad these butterflies had
    Was making collections of—boys.

There were boys of all sizes and ages
    Pinned up on their walls. When I said
'Twas a terrible sight to see boys in that plight,
    I was answered: "Oh, well, they are dead.
We catch them alive, but we kill them
    With ether—a very nice way.
Just look at this fellow—his hair is so yellow,
    And his eyes such a beautiful gray.

"Then there is a droll little darkey,
    As black as the clay at our feet,
He sets off that blonde that is pinned just beyond
    In a way most artistic and neat.
And now let me show you the latest—
    A specimen really select,
A boy with a head that is carroty red
    And a face that is funnily specked.

"We cannot decide where to place him.
    Those spots bar him out of each class.
We think him a treasure to study at leisure,
    And analyze under a glass."

I seemed to grow cold as I listened
To the words that these butterflies spoke.
With fear overcome—I was speechless and dumb,
And then with a start—I awoke!

We are glad this was only a dream; for we should grieve to see boys pinned up on the wall as much as the poet did, because we know it would hurt them. And killing with ether is not a nice way at all, when it comes to boys, for we know they should never be killed. They should be given the very best chance to grow up into strong, wise, good men. But if this dream helps any of us to understand that sticking with pins hurts butterflies, and other insects, and that there is no nice way of killing any of these harmless creatures because they also have a right to live, then it is a fortunate dream for us. To be mindful of the rights of a butterfly helps boys and girls to grow into better men and women. So we will thank Ella Wheeler Wilcox for helping us to see ourselves as others see us, because it helps us to understand the rights of these little creatures better. They are beautiful, winged things. Watch them among the flowers. Never try to touch them. Watch the motion of their wings! See them unwind their wonderful trunk and sip honey from the deep cups! It is wonderful, wonderful! In their happy summer life they will show you more beautiful things than poets have dreamed.

QUESTIONS.

What is the motto of this lesson?
What do we mean by seeing ourselves as others see us?
Where did the poet go in her dream?

What did the poet see?
Describe the different boys she saw on the wall.
How did she feel about it?
How did the butterflies feel about it?
What made such a difference in the way they looked at them?
Would any of you like to take the place of the butterflies and other insects, that are pinned up and killed with ether?
Is it fair then to treat butterflies so, just because you are large and strong and can do it?
Are you glad " The Butterfly Fad " is a dream?
How may the dream help us?
What are some of the rights of a boy?
What are some of the rights of a butterfly?
How may you learn most about a butterfly?
How long do butterflies live?
See how many new things you can learn by watching them.

CHAPTER X.
THE MOTHER RABBIT.
Carrie Shaw Rice.
"The Strong should help the Weak."

My cat, with the delicate, snowy throat,
   So staid and so steady of habit,
Now what have you brought from the field to-day,
   But a beautiful mother rabbit?

Just think of the little ones in their bed,
   All waiting for mother to feed them,
They'll wake in the night and cry in their fright,
   For mother who will not heed them.

Oh kitty! so shy and pretty,
   You wouldn't have done it, would you?
If you could have known of the babies alone,
   You couldn't have done it, could you?

They'll cuddle close in their nest alone,
   All night they will watch and listen,
Expecting to see through the dreaded gloom,
   Her brown eyes glimmer and glisten.

And now to look at her stiff and cold,
   In the sun on the threshhold lying,
While you look up with your innocent eyes,
   And wonder because I am crying.

For Oh, Kitty! so shy and pretty,
You wouldn't have done it, would you?
If you could have thought of the pain it has wrought,
You couldn't have done it, could you?

QUESTIONS.

What happened to the mother rabbit?
Describe the kitty that caught her.
Where were the little rabbits?
What happened to them?
Did the kitty understand what suffering she caused?
Could she understand it very well when her mistress told it over to her?

Can boys and girls understand all these things better than a cat?

Was it a sad thing that the mother was taken away and her little ones left to suffer and die?

Would it be far worse for a boy or a girl to take a mother rabbit, than for a kitty?

Would it be bad to take a little rabbit away from its mother?

Does the mother rabbit love her little ones and grieve to lose one?

If it is wrong to kill a mother rabbit, is it wrong to kill a mother bird or any other mother?

CHAPTER XI.
THE HUMMING BIRD'S WEDDING.
Love the Beautiful.

There was a big bush covered with pink roses. Two little girls stopped beside it and two little voices cried: "O how pretty?" Then two little hands picked each a rose and four little feet hurried away to school.

By the time the schoolhouse steps were reached one sweet rose was picked to pieces, chewed up and thrown away. But the other was placed in a slender vase on the teacher's desk, where it gave out beauty and fragrance all day and made fifty children better.

What a pity both roses couldn't have had a chance to do good!

A very wise poet, William Wordsworth, once said that the poorest little flower in all the world was so sweet and so beautiful that it made him glad until he was sad. Every beautiful thing is a blessing and we never should spoil a leaf.

Another poet, William Cowper, said he would not have a man for his friend who would kill a worm that did no harm, and he was right. Boys or girls that hurt the smallest thing or spoil the smallest plant, just for the sake of spoiling it, have put joy and blessing out of the world that they can never bring back.

A humming bird hummed in the rose bush and Louie ran to see. She did not touch, nor make a sound. She only peeped between the pink roses, and there on a spray with five pink buds she saw the wee'est bird on the dain-

tiest nest, with eyes like diamonds and a ruby-like throat. Louie was so gentle and careful that she never scared the beautiful, wee mother away, but watched her day after day
and learned many things. She had many a good look at the baby birds

(not much bigger than beans) and saw them open their hungry mouths.

She was almost as happy as the dear little mother, for she loved the beautiful and it made her glad and good.

One day, after she had found these rose-bush friends, her mamma read her the story of the "Humming Bird's

Wedding," which she liked so much that I am sure *you* will like it, too, so I give it here:

"THE HUMMING BIRD'S WEDDING"—MARY A. LATHBURY.

" A little brown mother bird sat on her nest,
  With four sleepy birdlings tucked under her breast,
  And her querulous chirrup fell ceaseless and low,
  While the wind rocked the lilac-tree nest to and fro.

" Lie still little nestlings! Lie still while I tell,
  For a lullaby story, a thing that befell
  Your plain little mother one midsummer morn,
  A month ago, birdies—before you were born.

" I'd been dozing and dreaming the long summer night,
  Till the dawn flushed its pink through the waning moonlight;
  When—I wish you could hear it once!—faintly there fell
  All around me the silvery sound of a bell.

" Then a chorus of bells! so, with just half an eye,
  I peeped from the nest, and those lilies close by,
  With threads of a cobweb, were swung to and fro,
  By three little rollicking midgets below.

" Then the air was astir as with humming bird's wings!
  And a cloud of the tiniest, daintiest things
  That ever one dreamed of, came fluttering where
  A cluster of trumpet flowers swayed in the air.

" As I sat all a-tremble, my heart in my bill,
  ' I will stay by the nest,' thought I, ' happen what will; '
  So I saw with these eyes by that trumpet-vine fair,
  A whole fairy bridal train poised in the air.

"Such a bit of a bride! Such a marvel of grace!
In a shimmer of rainbows and gossamer lace!
No wonder the groom dropped his diamond-dust ring,
Which a little elf-usher just caught with his wing.

"Then into a trumpet flower glided the train,
And I thought (for a dimness crept over my brain),
(And I tucked my head under my wing) 'Deary me!
What a sight for a plain little mother like me!'"

QUESTIONS.

What is the motto of this lesson?
What did the two little girls do with their roses?
How did the rose in the vase do good?
Was the one that was picked to pieces wasted?
Is it wrong to waste any good thing?
What did a wise poet say about the smallest, poorest flower?
How may one be so glad that he is sad?
Did you ever laugh till you cried?
What does another poet say about a man that will needlessly kill a worm?
Does it make boys and girls better to see beautiful things?
Does it make them better still to take care of beautiful things?
What did Louie see in the rose bush?
How did she happen to see so much?
What is the little brown mother bird's story?
Did she think it a great thing for a plain little bird to see so much beauty?
Did she love the beautiful? Do you?

CHAPTER XII.
THE SMALL LIFE OF SEA AND SHORE.
H. MARIE CURREY.

" Little Builders, build away—
Little Builders, build to-day!"

" How all the fishes are decked out—those glittering in plate armor, these only arrayed in their various colored jerkins, such as no Moorish artist could paint. How well clad are the insects; with what suits of mail are the crab and beetle, the bee and the ant furnished!"—*Theodore Parker.*

When we are inclined to look upon the various lower creatures with indifference, or contempt, and think it not worth our while to even consider what life or loss of life is to them; let us pick the smallest flower we can find and take prisoner a tiny gnat without harming so much as a hair of his head and put them under the microscope for better acquaintance. We will see what infinite care and love were bestowed on their creation, how the smallest parts are fashioned in grace and beauty, with nothing lacking to make their little lives complete. There is the shimmer of the rainbow in the little lace wing, and tints of sea shells in the wee petals. We will see, too, how frightened and distressed our prisoner is. How he exerts all his little strength to force an opening in his prison! Then we shall know that no created thing is insignificant and that life is dear to all, as it is dear to us.

It is because we are such strangers to the busy, thronging little people of sea and beach, that we have no fellow feeling for them and interest in them.

There is the retiring, quiet barnacle, who sleeps all through the ebb tide but wakes up at the soft touch of the first wavelet of the incoming sea, and very cautiously opens its house-door a little crack. If we are very still, we will see the door open wider and wider, and by and by a little hand will reach out, very timidly at first, but soon with confidence if no danger seems nigh. It is poetry of motion, the wave of that wee, brown hand, with its twelve graceful fingers moving in and out, in and out the little double door as Madame Barnacle takes breakfast.

The waves may wash, the sea-weed may even dash against the busy hand and the breakfast getting goes steadily on; but let us put a finger near, ever so quietly, and before it is touched that little hand is quickly drawn in, the house-door shut and securely locked. Nothing will open it either, except our superior strength. We might knock there all day and the lady of the house would steadily refuse to be at home to us. So we won't knock, since it is of no use, and it would be bad manners as well as unkind to keep a neighbor from breakfast, but we will wait at a respectful distance for one more look at the pretty hand.

It is some time before the door opens and it is with much more caution that the hand comes out. But if there is nothing to alarm, it soon resumes its busy work.

What a delicate sensibility! It is even beyond our own! What care and judgment used in self-protection! Surely that life must have been given for some good purpose and it cannot be right for us to take it without cause other than our own idle pleasure.

Then there is the self-asserting, bustling little crab, who shows such a brave and warlike spirit, till convinced there is real danger, when he takes to his ten heels and bids them carry him, with all speed, under something, a stone, a chip, a leaf, or into the hole in his enemy's shoe, if that is the nearest hiding place.

This fellow will furnish a never ending list of tricks and pranks to amuse and delight us.

We can truly say with Goldsmith:

"And still the wonder grew
How one small head
Could carry all he knew."

He can do something boys and girls can't. He can run just as fast and just as gracefully sidewise and backwards as he can forward. He can eat dinner with two big, awkward hands, whose fingers are all thumbs, and never get himself in a muss.

When his jacket and trowsers begin to feel a little too small he stores up, inside his body, material for a new suit. When he has enough on hand he takes off his old clothes and soon comes out in larger, prettier garments.

If some accident or some cruel enemy robs him of a leg he has the wonderful power to grow a new one in its place, and he doesn't limp a bit mean time.

The sand-hopper is the kangaroo of the beach. The muscles in his little hind legs seem as strong as the muscles in the legs of a good sized boy; at least he can out-jump the boy.

His coat of pale dove-color makes him nearly invisible among the gray pebbles of the beach. But if you move the stones carefully so as not to frighten him, you may see him shuffling along in the most awkward way. There is a great hump in his back and he looks as if the last thing he could do was to make a swift movement. But only point your finger at him and away he goes, so swift and so far you lose sight of him altogether.

We must not pass by the whelks and periwinkles without stopping to admire their pretty front doors. They are so brown and shiny, as if some skilled workman had just given them a hard oil finish. We can't help wondering where they carry the little file that so neatly opens the clam and oyster shells when Winkle is hungry and wants a little soup to eat. When we see them out of doors with all their pretty lobes filled out, then the greater wonder is "how they are ever to get back into their houses!"

When the day is warm and the water calm and clear there is no pleasanter pastime than watching the little fish of various kinds gambol about a quiet boat or some old moss and shell-covered log. Big fish eat little fish but not so here. It is a sweet lesson in peace and harmony to see how happily these various little races dwell together. Silver is as good as gold. He of the yellow skin, is as much respected as any. And let one playfellow be ever so freckled, he is never laughed at.

Their games of "Hide Go Seek" in and out the sea moss, and the tricks they play on one another, are enough to make old sober-sides laugh.

The favorite pastime of two little girls was standing barefoot in a clear brook to watch the minnows play about their ankles. It may be those foolish little fishes thought the four brown ankles were so many mammoth fishworms and they could swallow them whole. It seemed so, for with mouths wide open they repeatedly dashed their cold little noses against the bare legs much to the delight of the children. The game was, to stand so still that no little visitor would be frightened away and to see which pair of ankles would be visited by the largest fish.

This is only a hint of all the joy and delight that any bright-eyed boy and girl may find by sea and brook.

"THE SNAIL."—CHARLES LAMB.

"The frugal snail, with forecast of repose,
Carries his house with him wheree'er he goes;
Peeps out, and if there comes a shower of rain,
Retreats to his small domicile again.
Touch but a tip of him, a horn,—'tis well,—
He curls up in his sanctuary shell.
He's his own landlord, his own tenant; stay
Long as he will, he dreads no quarter day.
Himself he boards and lodges; both invites
And feasts himself; sleeps with himself o'nights.
He spares the upholsterer trouble to procure
Chattels; himself is his own furniture
And his sole riches wheresoe'er he roam;
Knock when you will, he's sure to be at home."

QUESTIONS.

What is the motto of this lesson?
Does that mean build true character every day?
Does true pleasure help to build true character?
If you live within reach of the sea, watch the barnacles feeding when the tide comes in and see what you can learn about them.
See how many interesting things you can learn about crabs.
Measure the distance a sandhopper jumps and see if a boy can match it.
What lesson do the happy little fishes teach?
Tell the story of the little girls and the minnows.
Tell the story of the snail and his house.

CHAPTER XIII.
KINDNESS MAKES PARADISE.

Sow seeds of kindness with an open hand,
And flowers of joy shall cover all the land.

An old Welsh fable tells us of a sweet girl whose heart was so true and kind, that it made her face lovely as the morning, and made her eyes shine like stars. The violets she carried did not wilt. The glad earth sent up a quatrefoil in her every footprint so that a tender grace of green marked her way.

All nature held her dear because her heart was kind and true and laughed for very joy at her bright coming. The fairest flowers kissed her feet and poured out for her their perfumes.

We cannot tell how long ago this story began to be told among the Welsh people. It was before they had books. Fathers and mothers told it over and over to their children. It was their fairy tale to teach that kindness makes paradise. The children loved it for its truth. They knew that the flowers and quatrefoils stood for joys and blessings and they passed the story on and on, till it became a part of their life and simple-hearted kindness marks that people to-day.

But the story of Eden is the sweetest of all the old, old stories. Milton beautifully tells us of the time when there was no wrong in the new fair world; when Eve walked through the lovely groves with her hand upon the lion's mane, and the timid fawn laid its head on Adam's knee and turned its large dark eyes up to his face with loving trust; when the birds came at his call and perched upon his hand to sing their sweetest songs. No living thing was scared to hear the step or voice of man, for "perfect love casteth out fear." Adam and Eve were never afraid of the tiger's claw or the lion's roar for again "perfect love casteth out fear." "Kindness makes paradise."

And still to-day kindness makes paradise. When playmates and friends are kind, the sun shines bright and our hearts are happy.

Henry David Thoreau, a great scholar, grew tired of the crowded city life and went into the woods to live by himself. He built a cabin by a little lake, and made friends with the fish and the birds and the beasts. "He fished without a rod and hunted without a gun." When the chipmunk came to get his beans, he treated him as a hungry neighbor and freely shared with him. When the squirrels had eaten up their winter stores, they came to him for nuts, and always found his latch string out. The timid partridge brought her downy chicks to pick beneath his window. Sparrows hopped upon his spade as he worked in the garden. Robin shared his breakfast, then perched upon his shoulder and rewarded him with sweetest song. And almost every creature of the wildwood came and received his kindness and caresses. His heart was warm and craved friendship, and they gave him sympathy that rested and refreshed him.

This is the story of Eden over again, and it is no fable. Among these chosen friends he studied and wrote his best books, and was very happy.

His books were full of noble thoughts, that have made the world better. But the best of all the good things he has given us, is the simple story of his life in the woods, and his kindly intercourse with the animals about him. He proved that to-day even, "perfect love casteth out fear."

Truly, kindness makes paradise for man and bird and beast.

QUESTIONS.

What is the motto of this lesson?
Tell the Welsh fable.

What does it teach?
Garden of Eden.
The quatrefoil is the four leaf clover and symbolizes good luck.
Were Eve and the lion friendly?
How did the timid fawns and birds feel toward Adam?
Were any of the animals in the garden afraid?
Were Adam and Eve afraid, even of the tiger?
Why were they so friendly toward each other?
Where did Thoreau make a home?
Did he find friends in the woods?
Do the wild creatures of the woods run to or from most people?
What made them come to him?
How did he treat the chipmunk?
How did he treat the squirrels?
Is the partridge usually wild or tame?
What did Thoreau's partridge do?
How did the sparrows and the robins show their friendship for him?
Is this a fable?
Did Thoreau write good books?
What is the best thing he has done for us?
What did his life by Walden pond prove?
What makes paradise in our hearts?

NOTE TO TEACHER.—Tell the children Milton's story of Adam and Eve with the animals in the Garden of Eden, and give them a full history of Thoreau and his life in the woods.

PART SECOND.

In which special effort is made to teach the right use of strength and wisdom and all good gifts; to teach the law of habit; to arouse and stimulate a sense of humanity, of honor, of justice, and of honesty in every detail of daily living and to continue the development of sympathetic interest and care of all forms of life.

CHAPTER XIV.
WHAT STRENGTH IS FOR.

"Oh, it is good to have a giant's strength, but it is tyrannous to use it like a giant."—Shakespeare.

Some of the old, old stories are of giants, not real men, just imaginary ones, whose heads touched the clouds as they walked, and whose tread made the earth tremble. They could tear up mountains with one hand and pull down stars with the other. They could step over seas and play with leviathans. But they were cruel and selfish with their great strength, using it to hurt, instead of help, mankind.

You see the meaning of the fable was that whoever had the advantage would use it selfishly and selfishness is always hard and cruel. Shakespeare makes the truth plain. Strength and power are *good* if they are put to *good uses*. The strongest arm should carry the heaviest load.

The men and women in the early days were like the fabled giants. The strong ones made the weak ones work for them. At last a very few came to rule over the rest. These rulers wore crowns and were called kings and queens. Some of them were kind and true, but many of them were false and cruel.

The people did not know how to help themselves. They thought kings were divinely appointed and that a man was sacred and noble just because he was king, no matter how bad he might be. The king thought so, too. He claimed most of the gold, silver and precious stones. He claimed the nicest things to eat, and drink, and wear, and all the most beautiful things to look upon. He selfishly heaped all these riches up in his palaces to go to waste while thousands and thousands of families starved.

But now we are learning more and more that "it is only noble to be good" and the world is happier and safer. Those old kings and queens had the giant's power and they used it like the fabled giants.

But the idea of true greatness has grown in the world, so that there are more people comfortable and happy to-day than ever before. This is because we are beginning to understand that we are all brothers; that the strong should help the weak; that if every one has peace and plenty, the greatest good has come to each of us. If there be giants they ought to carry the burdens of sick men, tired women, and little children.

Men and women are great indeed, when they become too noble to oppress any creature weaker than themselves. Strength and advantage are to do good with.

Did you ever see a boy set the dog on a cat?

What would he think of a man that would set a dog on his little sister?

Did you ever know a girl that forgot to feed her bird?

What would she think of the woman who forgot to feed a baby that could not ask for food?

Did you ever see a boy or girl scare a bird, stone a frog, run a cow, or jerk a horse?

What would you think of a strong man that would fall upon children wherever he found them, beat them, pull their hair, tear their clothes and count it fun, just because he could?

Boys and girls are giants to the animals about them.

Even the large, strong horse yields to a boy. Long years of training, the bit and bridle, and still more, something of devotion in the horse's spirit, gives the boy an advantage. Will he be *good* and *great* and use it for the blessing of this faithful friend? The big boy on the playground, that puts upon a little boy is rightfully accounted mean. Then isn't it mean for a boy to abuse an animal?

In an eastern fable it is told that Amurath, the Sultan, in a fit of anger struck a dog that was playing about his feet. A sudden peal of thunder was heard in the palace and the spirit Syndarac stood before him.

"Amurath," said he, "Thou has struck thine innocent brother, who, like thee, has received from the Almighty capacity for pleasure and pain. If thou art justified in giving pain to him, I, Syndarac, shall be justified in giving pain to thee."

"It is good to have a giant's strength, but it is tyrannous to use it like a giant."

Two boys were carrying a heavy basket on a rod between them. The older, stronger lad drew the basket nearer his end to lighten his brother's burden. He was big enough to be master and might have pushed it the other way, but he knew that "the strongest arm ought to carry the heaviest load" and better still, he *lived* it. In that he was great and good. Truly for such a one, "It is good to have a giant's strength."

QUESTIONS.

What does Shakespeare say about a giant's strength?
What are some of the old, old stories?
What is a fable?

In what were the kings and queens of early days like the fabled giants?

What is it to be noble?

What is true greatness?

To what are children giants?

What do you think of the big boy that plays the ugly giant?

What do you think of boys and girls that are tyrants to animals?

Tell the story of Amurath.

Tell the story of the two brothers.

Which do you like better?

CHAPTER XV.
TRUE COURAGE.

"The bravest are the tenderest, the loving are the daring."
—Bayard Taylor.

Sometimes people mistake cruelty for bravery. Bright and early one sweet June morning, Will set out with his bow and arrow, for a hunt. Into the orchard he went and soon spied a pretty robin perched on a topmost bough singing his morning song. Robin was so full of joy over the beauty in the wortd, that he did not notice Will aiming at his red breast.

Away flew the arrow, and the song ended in a cry.

Will did not stop to think of robin's dear mate left to feed the nestful of young ones all alone, but ran with the dead bird across the orchard to the sheep lot, where his little sister Daisy was feeding her pet lamb. He wanted to be praised, and tumbling over the fence in such haste that he was like to break his bow, he called: "See, Daisy! See! I got him the first shot! Ain't I a brave hunter?"

He talked so loud, and swung his boasted prize about so wildly, that little Daisy and the lamb were startled. So, too, were the grazing flock. They huddled together in their timid way, and then one big sheep stepped out as if to protect the rest, making dreadful threats with his horns.

Now was Willie's chance to be brave, but he only screamed and ran to the fence, leaving Daisy to be knocked over. He was bold to *give pain*, but not brave to *face danger*. His father called him a coward when he picked up bruised and frightened Daisy. The robin's mate, if she could have spoken, would have called him cruel.

Charles V, Emperor of Germany, was one of the ablest kings and bravest soldiers that ever lived. When danger threatened his country or his people, he was ready to face it; he knew no fear. One day in camp he was told that a swallow was building her nest upon his tent. He gave orders that it should not be disturbed. So the pretty nest, with its dainty, soft lining was finished, and soon the mother bird was sitting on her pearly white eggs. But before the young birds were hatched, the army had to break camp. The tents were struck except the Emperor's. He said: "Let it stand. .I can get another shelter, but she cannot for this brood. She trusted me for a home. I will not fail her." Surely the bravest are the tenderest.

Now hear this story of loving Tom and see how much he dared for the baby, one he loved best.

"TOM"—CONSTANCE FENIMORE WOOLSON.

[*From Humane Educator.*]

Yes, Tom's the best fellow that ever you knew.
Just listen to this:

When the old mill took fire, and the flooring fell through,
And I with it, helpless there, full in my view,
What do you think my eyes saw through the fire,
That crept along, crept along, nigher and nigher,
But Robin, my baby boy, laughing to see
The shining? He must have come here after me,
Toddled alone from the cottage, without
Any one's missing him. Then, what a shout—

Oh! how I shouted: "For Heaven's sake, men,
Save little Robin!" Again and again
They tried, but the fire held them back like a wall.

I could hear them go at it, and at it, and call:
"Never mind, baby, sit still like a man!
We're coming to get you as fast as we can."
They could not see him, but I could. He sat
Still on a beam, his little straw hat,
Carefully placed by his side; and his eyes
Stared at the flame with a baby's surprise,
Calm and unconscious, as nearer it crept,
The roar of the fire above must have kept
The sound of his mother's voice shrieking his name
From reaching the child. But I heard it. It came
Again and again. O God, what a cry!

The axes went faster; I saw the sparks fly,
Where the men worked like tigers, nor minded the heat
That scorched them—when suddenly, there at their feet,
The great beams leaned in—they saw him—then, crash!
Down came the wall! The men made a dash—
Jumped to get out of the way—and I thought
"All's up with poor little Robin!" and brought
Slowly the arm that was least hurt to hide
The sight of the child there—when swift at my side,
Some one rushed by, and went right through the flame,
Straight as a dart—caught the child, and then came
Back with him, choking and crying, but—saved!
Saved safe and sound!

   Oh, how the men raved,
Shouted and cried and hurrahed! Then they all

Rushed at the work again, lest the back wall
Where I was lying away from the fire,
Should fall in and bury me.

    Oh! you'd admire
To see Robin now; he's as bright as a dime,
Deep in some mischief, too, most of the time.
Tom, it was, saved him. Now, isn't it true
Tom's the best fellow that ever you knew?
There's Robin now! See, he's as strong as a log!
And there comes Tom, too—
     Yes, Tom was our dog.
 Truly "The loving are the daring."

QUESTIONS.

What does Bayard Taylor say about the brave and daring?
What do some people mistake for bravery?
What was Will's boast?
What did he do in time of danger?
What did his father call him?
What might the robin have called him?
What kind of a man was Charles V?
Read up his life.
How did he treat the swallow?
Did his tenderness spoil his courage?
How did Tom show his love?
Did it take courage and daring to rush into that burning building?
Do we admire courage in boys and girls?
If it is noble for them is it noble for a dog?
Repeat the motto in concert.

CHAPTER XVI.
THE BLUEBIRD AND THE SPARROW.

"'Tis only noble to be good.
Kind hearts are more than coronets."—Tennyson.

When Queen Esther was asked to risk her life to save her people, she hesitated. But when she thought of the thousands of men, women, and children she said nobly: "I go! and if I perish, I perish!"

She went, and the King was so touched by her soul-lit face that he held out the golden scepter and promised her the half of his kingdom. She saved her people and won higher honor for herself. But if she had lost her life in such service, it would have been a royal death worthy of the beautiful Queen. "'Tis only noble to be good."

A group of big boys in a certain school surrounded a bluebird and stoned it to death for noon sport. Big boys they were, as tall and strong as men, and they shouted as if it were a great victory when the little thing dropped to the ground, dead.

They had not yet learned that strength is a gift for noble uses. But they were covered with shame when the teacher showed them how unequal the contest was. Six to one! Six big boys, almost grown men, to one little bird! One defenseless, harmless songster that made the world more beautiful.

They might have made noon sport of helping a tired team of horses up the hill close by. They were strong enough to have put their shoulders to the wheel and made it play for all. And the driver would not have been obliged to unload half his wood. That would have been royal exercise indeed; but these boys worked off their extra energy by throwing sticks and stones to bring down a happy bluebird.

The teacher finishes her talk by reading from the board the schoolroom motto for that week.

" 'Tis only noble to be good.
Kind hearts are more than coronets."

Shame grew in their hearts as they realized how unequal the contest had been; how unworthily they had used their strength. They began to see that all gifts, that money, mind, influence, position, and strength are for good uses only. They could never do so mean a thing again. That was the best lesson of all the good lessons that teacher taught them. Noble uses make life noble.

"The meanest flower that blows
Has meaning that lies too deep for tears."
—*Wordsworth.*

Cowper, another English poet, says:

" I would not enter on my list of friends,
Though graced with polished manners and fine sense,
Yet wanting sensibility, the man
Who needlessly sets foot upon a worm."

We love and admire those who make the most of their position, and their gifts for the blessing of those around them. Even mean and selfish persons will cheer a brave, true action.

One evening a policeman discovered a sparrow fluttering about in one of the street lamps. Twilight was coming on. The poor bird had already nearly beaten its life out trying to get away. It still dashed desperately against the sides of the globe, falling back again and again, each time more bruised and helpless. The heart of the policeman was touched by that little struggling life, and he resolved to save it. There was no time to be lost, the electric current would be turned on soon. Hastily fetching a ladder, he mounted to the lamp and soon had the dusky brown bird in his hands. A glad shout went up from the crowd on the corner when it spread its wings and fluttered to the nearest roof.

The morning paper told the story, and that policeman was praised the city over. School children pointed him out to each other as " The good policeman." They well understood that " It is noble to be good."

Unselfish people are quick to relieve suffering wherever they find it. Selfish people think only of themselves.

One night a girl was awakened by the splashing sound of a mouse in her water pitcher. There was not water enough to drown the little fellow at once. He kept leaping up the rounding sides of the pitcher and falling back, leaping up and falling back! The girl was much worried that her sleep should be so disturbed, and at last rose and put the pitcher in the hall where she could no longer hear the continued struggle for life. It never occurred to her selfish thought that the mouse was suffering far more than she was and that it would be kind to drown him quickly.

This story of a boy in his teens, shows us a truly kind heart. One Sunday morning he saw a swallow in an unused room, beating against the window trying to get out into the sunshine. He hunted up the owner of the building, got the door open and patiently followed up the frightened bird till he caught it and set it free. It was too bewildered to find the way out by itself.

It is a beautiful thing to have such a kindly heart. So the Sunday school teacher thought when her most faithful pupil came in late and told of his morning work. She made it an object lesson to the class.

QUESTIONS.

What is the motto of this lesson?
What does it mean?
How did Esther show herself noble?
Do most people admire noble action?
Will a coward even cheer a brave deed and honor unselfishness?
Tell the story of the bluebird.
What did the teacher tell the boys?
What do you think of such an unequal contest?
What is strength for?
What might these boys have done for the woodman and his tired horses?
Are gifts of mind and body for good uses?
What is true use of our powers?
What is abuse of them?
Were the boys ashamed when they rightly understood their action?
Was this an important lesson for them?
Commit Wordsworth's lines.
Commit Cowper's lines.

Tell the story of the sparrow.
Did the policeman's kindness bring him praise?
What did the school children call him?
What is the first impulse of an unselfish person?
What is the first impulse of a selfish person?
Tell about the girl and the mouse.
What ought she to have done?
Tell the story of the boy and the swallow.
What use did the Sunday school teacher make of this incident?
What is it to be good?

CHAPTER XVII.
THE LAW OF HABIT.
"As the twig is bent the tree inclines."

The fibers of tow are slender and weak. A baby can break them in its play. But twisted into a rope they can hold a mighty ship to its anchor, and the giants of the storm cannot break it.

A good act repeated once is a slender habit that any child can break. But repeat it every day for years and it makes a character strong enough to hold a life to the anchor of right, and giants of evil cannot break it.

In the Mammoth Cave of Kentucky there are great pillars, white as alabaster. They are like beautiful strong arms holding up the immense roof. These pillars are built up little by little, day after day. Limestone rock, which was dissolved in water as common salt may be, trickled down through the ceiling, a drop at a time, and when one was hardened another came to join it. So its snowy beauty grew.

The wonderful star chamber in the same cave was spangled with splendor in the same patient way.

So beauty of character grows little by little, day after day, through words of truth and acts of love. Truth whiter than alabaster, and love stronger than the solid rock.

Many years ago, when our great Lincoln was a poor, young lawyer, he was riding in company with some distinguished judges and attorneys through an Illinois grove.

As they were hurrying on to reach the next town for the opening of an important term of court, they heard the cry of a little bird in the grass. Lincoln began to look for it. He was large and strong, so strong and so fond of exercising his strength that he was often called a giant. He

could lift a barrel of flour as easily as an ordinary man could lift fifty pounds. He could jump farther, run faster and lift more than any other man he knew. Best of all, his heart was big to match his body. From a boy, he
took the side of the oppressed and the weak. His mother could always count on his help. He was gentle and tender with all young things, and was always quick to answer any cry of distress. So now, he got down from his horse and soon had the unfledged birdling in his hands. His friends laughed at him, called him soft-hearted, and objected to such delay, for they were in a hurry. He told them to ride on, and began hunting for the nest. The little thrush had good use of its legs, if not of its wings, and had wandered far from home. It was a long hunt, but at last he had the pleasure of putting the birdling in the nest with its mates, and hearing the pretty brown mother

chirrup for joy. He felt paid for his troubles, even though he made all the rest of his journey alone. He reached the court room in time for his case, and was ahead by one kind act.

Another day, as he was riding across a swampy prairie, he came upon a half-grown pig, fast under a gate. The gate was over a mud-hole. The pig was covered with thick mud and struggling and squealing with all its might. Lincoln stopped and looked at it. He wanted to help the pig, but he had on his only good suit of clothes and was on his way to try an important case. He had no money to buy another suit. If he helped this dirty sufferer his clothes would be ruined and he would be unfit to go into the court room.

He was anxious to appear well at this particular time, so he rode on trying to think about his case. But his ears were full of shrill cries for help and he could think of nothing but that poor pig. At last his heart got the better of him, and he turned back and freed it, then hurried on, happier in spite of muddy clothes.

The habit of being kind to every living thing was so strong upon him, that he could not break it even for comfort and convenience. This habit grew stronger and stronger as the years went by so that when he was *president* and had a chance to liberate four million people he did it; did it in spite of the warnings of friends and the threats of enemies. Though he himself shrank from so dangerous an act, the cries of enslaved manhood, the moans of mothers and chilren urged him on, and he wrote the word that made them free.

It is true, the emancipation proclamation was a war

measure, but it was President Lincoln's great hearted sympathy that made such a daring measure possible. To-day he is loved by the truest and best men and women the world over, not because he was president of a great nation, but because he was good in a dangerous and trying time; because he thought of others instead of himself and bravely faced death to help the helpless. He was truly great because he was truly good. O, it is *good* to have a giant's strength when great wrongs are to be *righted!*

QUESTIONS.

What is the motto of this lesson?
How may the fibers of tow be broken?
What may they hold when twisted together and made into a big rope?
What of the strength of a good habit continued through years?
How are the wonders of the Mammoth Cave made?
How may beauty and strength of character be built up?
What was the great Lincoln called when he was a young man?
What kind of a heart had he?
What did he do for the little bird?
What did he do for the pig?
What did he do for four million slaves?
Why is he loved by so many?
Why is he great?
When is it especially good to have a giant's strength?

CHAPTER XVIII.

HONESTY.

**Beautiful faces have beautiful hearts!
Beauty is truth in the inward parts.**

" CATCHING BEAUTIFUL BECK "—MARIAN DOUGLASS.

With forehead-star and silver tail,
    And three white feet to match,
The gay, half-broken sorrel colt—
    Which one of us could catch?

" I can," said Dick; " I'm good for that."
He slowly shook his empty hat.
" She'll think 'tis full of corn," said he;
" Stand back, and she will come to me."

Her head the shy, proud creature raised,
As 'mid the daisy flowers she grazed;
Then down the hill, across the brook,
Delaying oft, her way she took;
Then changed her pace and moving quick,
She hurried on, and came to Dick.
" Ha, ha!" He cried, " I caught you, Beck!"
And put the halter round her neck.

But soon there came another day,
    And, eager for a ride—
" I'll go and catch the colt again;
    I can," said Dick, with pride.

So up the stony pasture lane,
And up the hill he trudged again;
And when he saw the colt, as slow
He shook his old hat to and fro,
" She'll think 'tis full of corn," he thought,
" And I shall have her quickly caught.
Beck, Beck!" He called; and at the sound
The restless beauty looked around,
Then made a quick, impatient turn
And galloped off among the fern.
And when beneath the tree she stopped,
And leisurely some clover cropped,
Dick followed after, but in vain;
His hand was ju-u-u-st upon her mane,
When off she flies, as flies the wind,
And, panting, he pressed on behind,
Down through the brake, the brook across,
O'er bushes, thistles, mounds of moss,
Round and around the place they passed,
Till, breathless, Dick sank down at last;
Threw by, provoked, his empty hat—
" The colt," he said; " remembers that!
There's always trouble from deceit;
I'll never try again to cheat!"

QUESTIONS.

What is the motto of this lesson?
Will truth in the inward parts show itself in honest dealing with every person and every creature?
Dick boasted that he could catch the colt easier than the

other boys and girls and he succeeded. How did he do it?

Why did "Beautiful Beck" come to him so promptly?

Did he promise her corn as much as if he had really spoken the promise in words?

Did he really lie to her?

Did she understand that he had lied?

The next time he called her and promised her corn, did she come?

Why did she gallop off?

Did she let Dick catch her when he had climbed the hill and was just upon her?

What kind of a chase did they have?

Did Dick have to give up at last, all tired out?

Did he understand then that he could not catch her because he had deceived her?

Commit what Dick says in the last two lines of the poem.

Was it wise, as well as honest, for him to resolve never to cheat again?

If he had been true the first time and given her corn, as he promised, would she have come up to him the second time?

Would it have saved him lots of hard work and trouble, as well as made him more respected, if he had been honest? Can you promise a thing by signs and looks, as well as by words?

If in any way you lead a person or an animal to expect anything of you, have you really promised it, though you have not said a word?

"Truth in the inward parts" means true in thought and word and deed. Does that mean fair in work and play?

If a boy jerks away from a fair catch and says, "I'm not caught!" Is he "true in the inward parts?"

If a girl looks in her book when she is to write an exercise from what she knows, is she "true in the inward parts?"

If one says: "I have watered the horse, I have fed the cow, I have cooped the chickens, or I have tended the birds," because these dumb mouths cannot tell that he has not; is he true in the inward parts?

Thoroughly learn the motto of this lesson and live it day by day.

CHAPTER XIX.
DOVETROT'S WAY.

Cynthia Fairchild Allen.

"**Kind words can never die.**"

It was a common sight—the faithful animal overloaded, pulling beyond his strength, the trembling limbs at last given out, and nothing but blows and shouts to reward him for doing his best.

"Shame on thee!"

The deep bass voice was heard with startling clearness from the group of men and boys who made up the usual spectators of such a scene.

"Shame on thee!"

The astonished Jehu dropped his arm to turn and see who it was that dared to interfere with him in the management of his "property."

"Just you mind your own biziness, 'n I'll tend to mine."

"This is my business, friend. It's the business of every man to see there's no injustice done his brother; all the more so if that brother be dumb."

"Well, Old Broadbrim, let's see 'thee' get thut 'oss up 'thout beatin' or yellin' ut 'im."

"You'd better not be sassy," sung out a small boy; "Dovetrot's got a star under his coat."

The man quieted down at once. He looked inquiringly at "Dovetrot," as the children unrebuked, called the good, broad-chested, not very tall old gentleman. His Quaker garb was dove-color, and a way he had of walking suggested the name "Dovetrot," by which he was familiarly known in the community. Dovetrot didn't deny the boy's statement, but looked at the brawny teamster with a quiet, steady eye that commanded respect.

All this time the fallen horse lay panting, with his limbs outstretched and trembling, and a look of despair in his eyes. Dovetrot got down on his knees to rub the aching joints, while, at the same time, he said to the man:

"Now do thee get a bucket of water, quick!" and to the poor beast he said, in soothing tones:

"Thee's got a hard master, poor boy; but may be we can make him better. Poor boy, good boy." He repeated this softly many times until the irritated nerves became qniet and the look of distress passed off."

"Now help him to drink," said Dovetrot, as the man brought the water; "and don't on any account yell at him or even speak rough to him. Your poor horse is as nervous as a child."

"Poor boy, good boy," repeated Dovetrot, soothingly, as he brought from one capacious pocket a tin basin and from the other a little bag of oats.

He put some water with the oats and held it under the horse's mouth. After eating, the poor beast's spirits continued to rise, and without any urging he soon got upon his feet.

The crowd cheered and the driver looked ashamed.

"Now, thee don't want to yell at thy faithful servant at any time," said Dovetrot kindly. "If thee will feel of his pulse before and after thee hast shouted at him in a cross way, thee will find it has jumped ahead at a gallopin' rate under thy harsh, hard tones. When it doesn't make him nervous and feverish, it makes him stubborn and ugly—like it does his brother, man. Horses don't like to be 'ordered around,' as the boys say. Why can't thee be polite to them when they are doing thee a favor? They are wonderfully kind and accommodatin'. They never haggle about what thee is going to pay them, but pitch right in and do their very best."

All this time Dovetrot was rubbing the horse's nose, and occasionally his knees and ankles, and almost whispering "poor boy, good boy."

"And thee seldom even thanks them," he resumed, to the driver. "Now come on my boy," in a cheery tone, to the horse, and the animal started his load—from before which Dovetrot had removed the stones, and followed his benefactor like a lamb.

A string of small boys brought up the rear, while the driver walked at the side holding the lines and looking as if he had found an idea.

The boys had witnessed scenes like this before, and one of their number had got up an impromptu song to the tune of "Kind Words Can Never Die." They now joined in singing this, probably for the twentieth time, stamping their feet as they danced along to emphasize the words, which we must confess had in them more truth than poetry:

> Kind words is Dovetrot's way,
> Quaker way, dressed in gray;
> Oats, words, and Dovetrot's way,
> Carry the day!

QUESTIONS.

What is the motto of this lesson?
What happened to the poor horse?
What kind of a driver did he have?
What did Dovetrot say?
What kind of a man was Dovetrot?
How did the driver treat him at first?
What did the small boy say?
What did the star mean?
Did the driver's manner change, and why?
What did Dovetrot do for the horse?
What did he have the driver do for him?
How did Dovetrot get the horse to go?
According to Dovetrot, how should a horse be treated?
What did he say about a horse's work and the pay he asks for it?
Was Dovetrot kind and considerate of the driver?
Were the boys interested in this mercy work?
Had they seen anything like it before?
What was their song?
Was Dovetrot's way a good way?
If Dovetrot had been rude to the driver would he have succeeded so well?
Are kindness and politeness important in all mercy work?

CHAPTER XX.
TRAPS.
AMOS HUNT.

"Do as you would be done by."

ABRIDGED BY PERMISSION OF THE AUTHOR, CYNTHIA FAIRCHILD ALLEN.

In a little hamlet among the Northwest mountains, where the capturing of fur bearing animals forms the chief employment of the inhabitants, lived Amos Hunt. In the winter season he gathered in quite an amount of money by his capture of the fur bearing animals.

It was the week before Christmas, and Amos was busy and happy for he was to go over the mountains and spend the holidays with his cousin, Julius Manning. His first trip so far alone, for he was but a lad. He had been over the route with his mother several times and knew it well. He had often set his traps near the same mountain path.

Let me describe these traps to you. They are made of semi-circular pieces of steel, so as to form a complete circle when open and fastened by a spring. The inside of each of these semi-circular pieces is supplied with a row of sharp teeth, and when the animal steps up to secure the bait, the trap springs, and one or more of his feet are caught and held fast by these sharp teeth. The trap is fastened to the ground by a stake, and almost always, in his struggle to escape, the poor captive tears the flesh off his feet or legs to the bone. Often the creature remains for hours and even days in this condition and the suffering he endures can hardly be expressed.

But Amos Hunt "never thought of this." And his mother and sisters evidently "never thought of it." His father before him had captured animals in this way, and probably *he* "never thought of it" either.

Amos concluded to mingle business with pleasure on that morning before Christmas. He had two traps set almost in the path of his journey, and he intended to take the animals he expected to find therein, to his cousin for a Christmas present.

As he neared his traps he discovered a fine mountain-brook-mink, struggling to escape from one of them. He grasped a stout stick and hastened to dispatch it, when suddenly he felt something clasp tightly around his ankle, and he was thrown violently to the ground. He had stepped into a trap that had been placed directly over the burrow of a mink, and his foot had slipped down through the trap when it sprung.

He did not feel anxious at first, for he supposed he would be able to get it off. But he had fallen over a prostrate tree in such a way that the chain of the trap caught on a broken branch and held his foot suspended in the air. Neither the branch nor the chain would give way and he could not lift himself up.

He was within ten feet of his captured mink, and after becoming wearied with his efforts to free himself, he turned his eyes toward the trembling creature that now in addition to the torture of the trap, suffered from the nearness of one whom the wild animal has learned to fear and dread.

Its broken leg was torn and bleeding, with its fruitless struggles to free itself. For the first time in Amos' life, pity took possession of his soul and he realized the cruelty he had so long been guilty of.

The little animal now and then uttered low, distressful cries, and a moisture like human tears filled its eyes. By and by Amos' ankle began to swell and the teeth of the trap pressed tighter and tighter. The moisture of pain stood out on his forehead in great drops, and he panted and trembled even as the innocent sufferer just beyond his reach.

All his ingenuity failed to contrive a means of relief, and he could see by the shadows that noon had come and gone. How his mother would have flown to his rescue if she had known! He shouted and called though he was almost certain that no ear could hear him in that lonely place. Despite his pain he ate of the lunch his good mother had given him and threw to the little mink such portions as he thought it might like. This at first frightened it more, but as it smelled food, after a time it began to nibble daintily, intermingling with its meal distressing cries that touched Amos to the heart.

"Poor little creature!" he said: "This may be a punishment for my cruelty. I know now how much my captives have suffered!" Then he tried to comfort himself by hoping it would live till some chance traveler passed and rescued them both, when he would nurse the little sufferer and make it well, and keep it if it would stay with him. As darkness settled down, the half human cries of his companion ceased and he could only imagine that it was dead. Would it be his lot also to die a slow death by exhaustion and torture?

As these gloomy thoughts passed through his mind, he heard a rustle in the bushes, then a well-known dog bounded past him. The master was not far behind, and Amos sobbed for joy.

"Hallo, youngster! What are you doing there? Stargazing with your toes turned up?" called the old hunter. He saw the trouble and immediately lifted Amos up in his arms and freed him. "Now mount my back," said the good friend, "and I'll carry you home."

"Wait a minute," said Amos. "I've a fellow captive out there in that trap. If he's dead, I want you to bury him right here, fur and all, for I'll never have money made from him, and I'll never catch mink or any other animal in that way again. If he's still alive I want to take him home." As the old hunter approached it, the little creature feebly moved. "He'll bite if he has life," said the man, hesitatingly. "Wrap it in my jacket," said Amos, with a voice and a look that made his friend take the little mink from the trap very tenderly, wrap it up and put it away in his big pocket. Then, with Amos on his back, they started homeward, the old dog leading the procession in lordly style.

It is needless to say that there was much coddling of Amos by mother and sisters, and that their sympathies were extended to the suffering mink at Amos' urgent request. Tibit, as he was thereafter named, at first objected to splints and bandages, but by and by he understood his friends and became very much at home with them. So, this family, that before had "*never thought*" about the suffering of animals, came to *think;* they thought to some purpose, and devised ways and means for new traps. After that, Amos, with Tibit in his pocket, roamed the mountain paths and set cage traps which caught his game securely and never hurt it.

A trap that is just as cruel as the one in which the little mink was caught, is the steel rat trap. Many a poor rat is held helpless and in pain for hours before it is taken out and killed. We must prevent the use of such traps as far as we can, either for wild animals or for those that trouble our houses and stables. Every creature that must be killed, can be killed in a merciful way.

A good trap for vermin of house and field is a platform lightly balanced over a vessel of water, so that when the creature walks out on it for the bait, he is tipped into the water. Drowning is an almost painless death.

QUESTIONS.

What was Amos Hunt's work in winter?
What kind of traps did he use?
Were they cruel traps?
Are such traps in common use?
Why did Amos use such a cruel trap?
Did his mother and sisters think about the cruelty of them?
Had his father before him thought of it?
What made Amos think at last?
What made his mother and sisters think?
What did they do to make it better?
What kind of a trap did Amos use after he was caught?
Did it catch and keep his game surely?
What was its great advantage?
Is any trap that hurts an animal and does not instantly kill it, cruel.
Should mice and rats and other creatures that trouble about the house and barn, be killed mercifully?
Is it important that anything that is to be killed should be killed quickly and mercifully?

CHAPTER XXI.
FISH AND HARMLESS REPTILES.

Abriged from a leaflet published by The Humane Education Committee, Providence, R. I.

"We do pray for mercy, and that same prayer
Doth teach us all to render the deeds of mercy."—Shakespeare.

A Wise Fish.

How do I know so much? I will tell you. I am an old fish now, and have been caught three times myself. The first time I was a mere baby, and was taken into the hands of a tall man with a kind face, who said: "Poor little fish; you are too small to eat, and you are not hurt, for the hook is only caught in your lip, and I will take it out very carefully. *If you were badly hurt I would kill you at once;* but there, you are free now to swim away and forget all about me." But I never did forget him, and if I must be eaten, I wish it might be by that man. The next time I was caught by a woman, who swung me into the air and dashed me among the rough rocks, screaming for some one to take me off. But my head was caught in a rock and the hook was jerked away, taking a piece of my jaw with it, and I fell into the sea. Lastly, I was caught by a boy, who called me "such a beauty," for I was full grown by that time. Had he known how to kill me quickly, I would have made him a good dinner; but he threw me into a hollow in the rocks, as he had seen others do, and soon the friendly ocean sent a big wave which washed me back home again.

Boys and girls, we hope that you will not catch fish "for fun," but only when you think you need them to eat, and that then you will kill them *at once*. If you should catch any that are too small for use, but which are badly hurt, kill them also, and do not throw them back into the water to suffer.

"Agassiz always taught his pupils to kill fish as soon as caught, by a blow on the back of the head, that they might not suffer before dying. Such fish keep better, and are better to eat; and the best fishermen in Europe and America always kill their fish as soon as they catch them. Humane persons kill fish-worms and other bait instantly by plunging them in a dish of boiling water."—*Geo. T. Angell.*

AQUARIUM FISH.

In China, the little goldfish, a native of that place, is treated better than in England and America, being placed in china bowls, which have holes made at the bottom as places of shelter. Even in our glass bowls such places might be provided and some suffering prevented.

"Fishes cannot be kept in health and comfort for any length of time except out of doors, in running water, or water at least exposed to the influence of sun and air, with rain. Those who take the charming little minnow or any other of the pretty little fishes and condemn them to an 'aquarium' are sentencing the creatures they profess to be fond of, to a slow, cruel, lingering death. Half of such captives die for want of rest; they are chased and terrified to death; you see them moving round and round their places of captivity till they die, because they want a place of refuge. They cannot beat against their prison walls, or flutter, or cry as a bird does; their misery is silent, but in reality it is the same, though in a lesser degree. For all fish must have (all the more because they do not sleep), darkness to sooth them, rest and quiet. Their eyes are not formed to endure the light all round them. No wonder that they dash from side to side when first placed in such a thing, plunging and struggling vainly to escape, trying to bury their heads in imaginary mud which they hope to find at the bottom—knocking vainly against the cruel clearness which they cannot swim through. How awful to be exposed to the full glare of sunlight without eyelids or hands with which to cover your face?

"It is a dismal sight to see glass prisons in which the exquisite little goldfish is doomed to go gasping round and round—breathing twice as fast as he would do in his native pond or river, because he cannot get oxygen enough in his close quarters. He grows thinner and thinner day by day, till his poor little body can no longer keep its balance, but begins to be buoyed up sideways, like a dying crocus flower blown by the wind. At last the glimmering corpse lies motionless, floating on the top of the water which has filled his bowl. He has been dying slowly there ever since he was placed in it; now his sufferings are over; mute, dull, dim as his senses may have been, they were filled with sorrow and discomfort all his tiny life, instead of with the pleasure that God made him to feel. His jailers laid pains upon him such as he was able to know—though they may have admired and even loved the wee golden thing, they loved their own amusement better."—*Edith Carrington, in "Workers Without Wage."*

HARMLESS REPTILES.

Many of our common non-venomous snakes are exceedingly useful in destroying noxious insects (such as ticks and beetles) as well as rats, mice and gophers. The chicken snake is one of these.

"Though not venomous, the blacksnake fights and destroys the more sluggish rattlesnake."

The gartersnake "feeds upon larvæ and wood ticks."

The *petyophis bellona* is a very common and important Western form of the pinesnake or bullsnake of the East. It "is not only harmless, but exceedingly useful as a vermin destroyer."—*C. W. Green, M. D.*

Frogs and toads are certainly entitled to our protection on account of the good they do in destroying vast numbers of insects and worms. The toads do this in the gardens and the frogs in marshy places, where the air, on account of flies and other insects, would be almost unfit to breathe without the services they render.

"WHAT DID WE CATCH?"—KATE KELSEY.

When we went fishing, Maud and I,
Within the shadowed waters nigh
The mossy bank, that summer day,
The speckled trout in safety lay.

What did we catch? You ask in vain,
If all the angler has to gain
Is trophy of the hook and line—
Then ask his comrades home to dine.

We caught a glimpse of summer skies,
And as we watched a skylark rise

From out the azure depths so fair,
We caught the song that thrilled the air.

The fragrant breath of tall pine trees
We caught from every passing breeze,
And in the waters, calm and clear,
The trout flashed by without a fear.

What did we catch? The joy of life,
And freedom from all care and strife;
We caught the smile on Nature's face,
In that enchanted happy place.

O! many days have passed away
Since Maud and I that summer day
Caught hope and joy and visions fair,
And left the trout to Nature's care.

QUESTIONS.

What is the motto of this lesson?

Tell the story of the wise fish.

When and how should fish be killed for the sake of mercy and for the sake of good food?

What should be done with fish that are too small for food, if they are hurt by catching?

Was the man's treatment of the little fish that was unharmed, both wise and kind?

Is it wrong to fish for sport?

Is it wrong on the fisher's account, as well as on account of the fish?

What are George T. Angell's directions for preparing bait?

Look up Agassiz?
Was he very wise about fish?
What are necessary conditions for the health and comfort of fishes?
Can fish have sufficient air in small aquariums?
Can they get rest and shelter from the light, sufficiently in glass vessels?
Is it right to sentence these little creatures to a lingering death for our pleasure?
Are their eyes formed to endure light all around them?
Name the harmless reptiles mentioned here.
Name the harmless reptiles of your vicinity.
Find out all you can about the wide spread, harmless gartersnake.
How does it help the gardener and the farmer?
What venomous reptile does the blacksnake destroy?
Where are toads special helpers?
Where is the frog's special work?
Is it good business, as well as good heart, to protect these helpful, harmless creatures?
Commit the poem "What Did We Catch?"
Did they catch something better than fish?

NOTE TO TEACHER—Make clear the difference between small house aquariums and large basin or pools with running water in a yard or park.

CHAPTER XXII.
PETS.

"Evil is wrought by want of thought as well as want of heart."—
Thomas Hood.

There are almost as many pets in the world as there are people. So it becomes important for us to study about them, that we may understand their claims on us as well as our claims on them.

It would be a dreadful thing to forget to give a baby food because it could not ask for it. Mothers will not let themselves forget just because the little ones are so helpless. Then is it not cruel to neglect dumb animals, and leave them to suffer from cold, and thirst, and hunger, just because they can't tell us what they want? Can it be a good excuse for such neglect to say, "I didn't mean to; I forgot; I didn't know."

Since cruelty is the worst thing in the world, it is worth while for us to study carefully the rights and needs of the beings about us, whether they be human or dumb, and be mindful of them. It is well for us to *mean* to do right, but it is not worth much to others, unless we *do* it.

A boy gave a pail of brine to his pig, not knowing the danger. This sleek, white pig was his pride. Under his training it had learned many interesting tricks, and was quite the wonder of the neighborhood, being called the performing pig. The petted creature drank the brine eagerly, and was soon dead.

It did not comfort the unhappy master to remember that he "*didn't know.*" Bitterly he wished that he *had known* in time to save his pig. "Cruelty is wrought for want of thought as well as want of heart."

So kindness prompts us to a careful study of the rights and needs of those who cannot ask for what they want.

Man has power over the beasts of the field, the birds of the air and the fish of the sea. He has tamed the lordly lion with his eye, and made the huge elephant his faithful servant. The horse waits patiently upon his will, and the dog became so early attached to human companionship that all trace of his wild life is lost, except the way he turns around to lie down. Naturalists say this is the way he made room for himself in the tall grass when he was in the wilderness, before he knew a master. There are no wild dogs now, and never have been since history began. It is the same with cats; they have no wish to live apart from men.

The wild creatures are very happy in orchard and meadow, on the plains, in the forest and among the mountains, so happy that whoever watches them in their glad free life grows happier. The squirrel in the tree, the sea gulls feeding on the beach or buffeting the storm, the antelopes, unscared, flying over the hills with winged feet, speak joy in every movement. It is much better to leave them free, but if they are tamed, put in cages or parks, or made free household friends, they become very dependent on their human companions, and a day's neglect, a harsh word, or a rude blow may cause them great suffering. These friends in feathers and fur are very sensitive. An ugly look will throw a sensitive horse into a fright, and a rough movement will send a panic through a flock of sheep.

Cats and dogs show by many signs that they crave attention and affection as much as children do.

In one happy family, when the children's hour came and they climbed on their father's knees and were cuddled close in his arms for lots of heart love, Watch, the house dog would come too, and crowding his nose in next to his master's breast, would whine and beg to be petted also. No little one of the group (there were many of them) was happier than he in the tender caresses of that loving father. He wagged his tail till it wagged his whole body, and barked in an ecstacy of delight. The children said that was his way of laughing. They cheered and laughed, too, then hugged their father and Watch together. Watch loved them all very much and was faithful in their service. He was as mindful of the baby as a big brother. When baby was learning to stand, he thought it was great fun to pull himself to his little feet by whatever he could lay hands on. Sometimes, as faithful Watch stood beside him, he would get tight hold of his slick coat and raise himself up. Baby was heavy and Watch was not a large shepherd, but he would brace himself and stand firm till the crowing, laughing little one was well upon his feet. His patience never gave out while the happy baby clung to him for support, but he would not let the older ones impose upon him. He enjoyed play as much as any child, and generally made one in the outdoor games, but he would turn quickly from any sport or would leave his dinner for a word or a pat from his master.

Such a faithful, loving creature, has rights that even a baby should learn to respect. To leave him hungry and thirsty, to give him cross words or blows, would be mean and cruel. No one lets the baby hurt his little sister because he does not understand that his scratches and blows and hair pulling hurt. We take his hands away and protect the little sister. Soon baby learns better. We should teach him in the same way to respect the cat and dog. It is wrong to let him abuse them. It hurts them as much as it hurts the little sister, besides making baby cruel.

It helps to take the selfishness out of almost any heart to rightly care for something alive. Let us be sure that we *do rightly* care for these friends we make so dependent upon us. Cats and dogs have been with men so long they have no wish to go back to a wild life. The great philosopher, Comte, says that we have made them partakers of our humanity. Let us look to it that we make them partakers of our *best humanity;* that we share our *virtues*, not our vices, with them.

Never excuse neglect of any creature with the words: "I forgot!" Remember that to forget is selfish, and selfishness is sin.

QUESTIONS.

What is the motto of this lesson?
Are pets common?
Is it well for boys and girls to have pets?
How does right care of animals help us?
Have almost all the higher animals been more or less tamed?
What animals have lost all knowledge of their wild life?
Would it be cruel to turn the dog into the wilderness to live now?
Would it be almost as hard on a cat to desert her?
Are animals sensitive to kindness?
Tell the story of Watch and the happy family.
Should a baby be allowed to hurt such a friend, because it does not know better?
Should we be careful to feed and water our pets?
Why should we?
Is "I forgot" a good excuse?

CHAPTER XXIII.
FRIENDS OF SCHOOL AND HOME.

"Kindness is the Outward Expression of Inward Grace."—Lydia A. Irons.

One teacher tells us of a stray cat adopted by her school that became a most coveted reward of merit. The boy or the girl whose deportment was one hundred, and whose lessons were mastered, might have kitty for a desk mate a little while. Gentle manners became more habitual among the children, for public sentiment was hard on any one that offered puss a rudeness, and they could not in reason be less kind to each other than to a cat. So the standard of morals grew among them.

Another teacher established a snailery in her room and many were the happy lessons learned from these novel pets. The baby snails were objects of tender interest, and every life became precious in the pupils' eyes.

A country school was surprised one morning by the announcement from a Jenny Wren that she meant to neighbor with them. One shutter chanced to be closed, and she hopped through a broken slat with a twig in her mouth. After turning her head from side to side, and eyeing the entire school through the glass, she decided that that window sill was the very place she wanted for a nest. For her to decide was to act, and within two weeks Jenny was sitting on a nest full of eggs. She became the pet of the happy school. Under the teacher's good guidance they scattered crumbs upon the window ledge, so that her daily bread came without much toil. Of course the shutter was never moved; but as the pleasant acquaintance lengthened and the warmer days came on, the window was raised and Jenny looked upon the bright faces with full content. When the little birds were all hatched—one, two, three, four—it was hard to tell which was the proudest, the mother wren or the school. When feeding time came that nest full of mouths was the center of interest. Teacher and pupils were helped in their work by the nearness of this happy family. There was never a rude word or touch to disturb the friendship on either side. One of the smallest members of that school, now grown, and with a little girl of her own in school, told the story with a remembered pleasure that made music in her voice. "Lie low at the feet of beauty, that ever shall abide."

Ernest Ingersoll charmingly tells of his pet squirrels. They were pets in the only right way for these and all other freedom loving creatures. They accepted his favors and gave him their confidence, but were at perfect liberty to work out their own sweet wills in the wideness of outdoors. He and his friend, the doctor, placed boxes in the trees for them and fastened poles from tree to tree for connecting bridges, extending lines to their own window sills. Here is his charming description of their play. From *Harper's Magazine*, copyright, 1892, by Harper & Brothers, March number: "One morning, the middle of October, I observed that a family of four young squirrels was venturing forth from a box just outside my study window; their prime characteristic was inquisitiveness. What a fine and curious new world was this they had been introduced to! How much there was to see! How many delightful things to do! They ceaselessly investigated everything about them with

minute attention, and had very pretty ways, such as the
habit of clasping each other in their arms. They fre-

From Harper's Magazine.   Copyright, 1892, by Harper & Brothers.

quently scratched and stroked one another. Once I saw
one diligently combing another's tail with his fore feet.
Young red squirrels, of which we had also a family or two,
play somewhat differently, having a peculiar way of regu-

larly boxing with their fore paws. Gradually they gained strength and confidence, and then you will see how far the liveliness of the young can surpass even the tireless activity of the old squirrels. Both old and young are exceedingly fond of play, springing from the ground as if in a high-jumping match, and turning regular summersaults in the grass; but the most amusing thing is this, finding a place where the tip of a tough branch hangs almost to the ground, they will leap up and catch it, sometimes with only one hand, and then swing back and forth with the greatest glee, just like boys who discover a grapevine in the woods or a dangling rope in a gymnasium. These, and many similar antics, seem to be done "just for fun." It took our squirrels a very short time to learn that cracked nuts of several varieties, grains of corn, and other food were to be had on the window sill. The squirrels know furthermore that the nuts are placed there from the inside, and if, as occasionally happens, the sill is empty, they will often stand up and tap upon the glass, as if to attract notice to their hunger. Moreover, they know very well when meal hours come around, and will present themselves at the windows pretty regularly, since they have learned to expect more than ordinary attention then, even when the meal is occasionally omitted, so that no noise of preparation could have apprised them of the time. The doctor has had a fèw come timorously to take corn from his fingers. * * * *

"It is plain that they recognize all of us as acquaintances from their indifference to our presence, while they will raise a great clamor when a stranger walks about under the trees. They will stay quietly eating on the window sill, while one of us sits just inside the glass, but if they see a visitor in the room will almost invariably seize a nut and scamper away as fast as they can go.   *   *   *   In winter they are more active, if anything, than in summer, racing about the trees at a furious rate, as if invigorated to fresh activity by the keen air."

This nature study was worth while, and these pets were ideally treated. If we would make friends with such wild creatures, we should observe the ordinary social delicacy that never offers a hand that is not welcome. Sympathetic nearness cannot be forced; it must be won.

But cats and dogs, and our barnyard friends of stall and shed, delight to come much nearer to us and give us closer affection than any of these. There are many pretty tricks that even a child may teach them, that add pleasure to their lives and ours.

A boy I knew had a kitty that would jump through his arms, or through a hoop held high from the floor. He taught her this by beginning to put his arms about her on the floor, drawing them in close and saying: "Jump, kitty, jump." The crowding in of the hands upon her made her step over. Then he would pet her and try it again, taking care not to weary her with too long practice at a time, and always saying the same words in the same way. Some cats will drink milk out of a goblet or pitcher by dipping the paw in and licking it off, and never so much as spill a drop. But I think this is an art acquired by themselves, or from suggestions among themselves. Cats are much more teachable than many suppose. Their extreme shyness and sensitiveness hinders them from ready performance in public.

A dog delights to please his master, and so is always in a teachable attitude. A little boy and girl of ten and twelve taught one of their dogs to draw a little milk wagon, and to help them in their work of delivering milk in a small town. Pedro became very bridlewise, could back and turn as skillfully as a horse. When asked the secret of their success, they answered promptly that it was because they began with him when he was a pup. They tried training an old dog but he didn't learn much. How dogs are like people!

A horse will sometimes follow his master like a dog. Some are more affectionate than others. I know a horse named Prince that in a strange place clings to his master much as a timid child clings to its mother. One day he took his master and mistress a journey of several miles to a farm he had never before visited. After a feed of grain he was turned out to graze. He was eager for the sweet grass and fell to eating at once, but before his master reached the house he heard the sound of hoofs behind him, and, looking back, saw Prince hurrying to catch up with him. The horse came up and rubbed his head against his master as if to say, "Don't leave me alone." Again he was put back in the pasture and his master stopped just over the fence, in full view, talking with his friend the farmer. Prince fed contentedly until the two men, in examining some trees, passed out of sight. When Prince looked up, and could not see his master he began to gallop up and down the fence neighing loudly. His master whistled to him and he was satisfied again. It was enough to know that his best friend was near.

There can hardly be a more winsome pet than a little lamb. A calf has its attractions.

One girl had a beautiful, silver laced Wyandotte rooster trained to come at her call and jump upon her shoulder, but the most ideal group I recall was a handsome boy just in his teens with a pure white dove on each shoulder. They were billing and cooing against his face between the pecks after the wheat in his hands. There was evidently the sweetest friendship all around.

QUESTIONS.

What is the motto of this lesson?
Tell the story of the school's pet cat.
How did the snailery help in another school?
Tell about the pet wren of the country school.
How did they keep up such a good friendship on both sides?
Were teacher and pupils helped by this neighbor, and, if so, how?
Tell the story of Ernest Ingersoll's pet squirrels.
Did they distinguish between friends and strangers, and how?
How did they prove that they could measure time?
Did Mr. Ingersoll learn more about squirrels and have more pleasure from these pets than he could have done if they had been shut in a cage?
Is the friendship of these happy, wild creatures forced or won?
Is it crime to shut them up?
Can they teach us so much or please us so well?
Are there animals that like to come closer to us?

What are some of the most familiar pets?

Tell the story of the loving cat? How did her master teach her to jump through his arms and through a hoop?

Tell about the bridlewise dog?

When was his training commenced?

Is it important for animals and people, too, to begin to learn useful and pleasant things when young?

Tell the story of Prince.

May a chicken become a real pet?

See how many interesting incidents of chickens can be given from the personal knowledge of the pupils?

What other animals make pleasant friends?

Are pigeons affectionate?

CHAPTER XXIV.
A CAGED LARK.

"Poor liberty is better than rich slavery."—Beecher.

Some one has said: "If a man becomes a Christian, his horse will be the first to find it out." Until Thoreau tried it, no one supposed that animals of the wildwood could be tamed by kindness, though it has long been known that successful horse trainers and keepers in menageries succeed through *kindness* and *honesty*. Even dumb animals like to hold a man to his promise. The dog that has been deceived is never after so trusty. Like begets like. Trust begets trust.

This was the great secret of Thoreau's charm. He loved and trusted his friends of feathers and fur and was a good providence to them. They understood that he was greater than they, and in many pretty ways showed they thought that by right, the strong should help the weak. Not a creature in the forest was afraid of his power, because he never failed to use it for their blessing. So everything had faith in him and loved him as being great and good. He was "monarch of all he surveyed, was lord of the fowl and the brute."

"There is nothing so kingly as kindness,
Nothing so royal as truth."

A few harsh words would have made all those timid creatures run from him and the loneliness of the wildwood would have been more than he could bear.

The freedom of these pets is their greatest charm to

those who read the story of Walden pond. And we can not doubt that the squirrels and the birds were far happier, free to come and go at will, than they could have been in gilded cages.

Lydia A. Irons, Athol, Idaho, has an ideal aviary. It takes in the wideness of outdoors, and the birds make freewill offerings of themselves.

By means of cups and plates on a stand in her front yard, she has established a drinking fountain and a free bath. Thither hundreds of the feathered tribes flock each day. After a drink and a splash, they rest upon perches put up expressly for them by the house windows, and plume themselves and sing out their ecstacy of love and thanks.

From "Our Home Pets." Copyright, 1894, by Harper & Brothers.

They fly away and gladden many other hearts with their sweet melodies, but this is their rallying ground day after day.

Think of it! Not one bird, but hundreds! Not held behind bars, but self-bound with silken cords of love and trust that sweeten all their freedom.

Every boy and girl may have such pets and grow more beautiful in face and life. Every school may have such an aviary. Try it! The little service of carrying water to fill up the oft emptied plates and cups will be a coveted pleasure, and your joy in this kind of free friendship will equal the birds.

"The love of liberty with life is given."

Every creature of field, and wood, and stream, loves its liberty as you will soon know by watching.

Study carefully the poem of the prisoned lark, commit it and you will be ready as the poet to fight for its freedom. Wage a peaceful war. Teach! Persuade! Begin with yourself and never take from these happy children of nature their rightful liberty.

A Caged Lark.

[From Chamber's Journal.]

A cruel deed
It is, sweet bird, to cage thee up
Prisoner for life, with just a cup
And a box of seed,
And sod to move on barely one foot square,
Hung o'er dark street, midst foul and murky air.

   From freedom brought,
And robbed of every chance of wing,
Thou couldst have had no heart to sing,
   One would have thought.
But though thy song is sung, men little know
The yearning source from which those sweet notes flow.

   The selfish man!
To take from thee thy broader sphere,
Where thousands heard thy music clear.
   On Nature's plan;
And where the listening landscape far and wide
Had joy, and thou thy liberty beside.

   A singing slave
Made now; with no return but food
No mate to love, nor little brood
   To feed and save;
No cool and leafy haunts; the cruel wires
Chafe thy young life and check thy just desires.

   Brave little bird!
Still striving with thy sweetest song
To melt the hearts that do thee wrong,
   I give my word
To stand with those who for thy freedom fight,
Who claim for thee, that freedom, as thy right.

QUESTIONS.

What is the motto of this lesson?
Tell what it means.
If a man is good will his horse know it?

What is the great secret of successful trainers of animals?
Do animals seem to recognize a higher power in man?
How was it in Thoreau's case?
In what respect was he like Robinson Crusoe?
What is it to be kingly and royal?
Give the line from Dryden.
Does that mean that birds and squirrels love liberty?
Did Thoreau's pets give more pleasure and enjoy more than they could have done caged?
Tell about Lydia A. Iron's birds.
Might every home and school have an aviary?
In the poem, "A Caged Lark," what losses and privations are spoken of in the first stanza?
Would it be easy for you to sing, and be happy, under such privations?
Does the poet think the lark yearns for its lost liberty?
How many hear the song when the lark is in the fields?
How many hear it when it is in prison?
Is this a loss to the sum of happiness?
What does the poet call the bird in the fourth stanza?
Why does he call it brave?
Is it a good thing to make the best of things, and give and get what good we can?
What does the poet promise to do in the last stanza?
Will you help the poet?

PART THIRD.

In which detailed care of common domestic animals is taught so far as pertains to their economic value, comfort, and the reflex moral influence on man, along with matters of general interest that may tend to create a greater feeling of responsibility and sympathy for the creatures we have made dependent upon us.

CHAPTER XXV.
CATS.

H. MARIE CURREY.

Study to forget *not one*, save *self*.

The cat is the most common animal we have. Nearly all boys and girls have at some time in their lives possessed one. But no pet has been so misunderstood or so badly treated as poor kitty.

We never teach her good manners while she is young, as

we do the dog; yet if she gets into mischief she falls into disgrace, and everybody is ready to cry "scat," and take part in chasing her from the house, till she is frightened and timid. She is never sure when a hand is raised whether it is to strike or stroke her.

A kind man, I know, who likes to have cats about his house and barn, for the good they do as well as for their pretty ways and pleasant friendship, takes great pains that they shall be taught what is right while they are young and can learn easily. If the kitties attempt to get into the milk pail they are taken up and very kindly and gently punished right near the pail; then, after being taken a short distance away, are soothed and petted before they are put down.

If they get on the table, they are punished right there, then taken off and stroked till their fear is gone. Cats are so sensitive, harsh treatment is *never* necessary. You would be surprised to see how quickly they learn when kindly taught.

These cats will sit by a bucket of fragrant new milk and wait for their pan to be filled, never touching the forbidden bucket. If a little patient waiting is not soon rewarded, they hunt up some member of the family and ask for milk in the most intelligent way, by peeping in their empty pan and then running to the bucket, all the time uttering soft mews that say so plainly "See, I am waiting for my breakfast."

One thing this good friend of cats never forgets, and that is, that they get hungry and thirsty, just as people do. He never drives them to thieving habits by neglecting to feed them. None of us forget our own dinners, but many,

many times we forget or neglect poor kitty, and perhaps put her roughly out of doors if she annoys us with repeated asking.

Many people think cats will not catch mice if well fed and that therefore sleek cats are not so valuable. This is a great mistake, for mousing is their instinct. Starvation weakens their sense of smell, so they cannot do their work as well. If cats catch a good many mice, milk is almost a necessity to keep them in good health. Otherwise they thrive on cooked vegetables and a very little or no meat. Grass and catnip should be given now and then, if they are not where kitty can help herself. No matter how much milk a cat has, she needs water; in warm weather she needs it often. There should always be a basin of clean water within her reach.

It is a good thing to remember that mice are nocturnal in their habits. So if you expect kitty to catch them you must give her the freedom of the house at night. If a pan of fine, dry earth is put in a convenient place she will never be untidy about the house.

It is cruel to let tabby lie by the warm stove all day, and then put her out at night unless you provide a warm and sheltered nest; even then she will suffer if the weather is severe. Cats are very sensitive to cold.

Cats are much more useful than dogs in ridding a place of rats. These vermin soon leave premises where they are hunted by cats, but have been known to increase rapidly where terriers were used.

Let us put ourselves in kitty's place and try to understand the cruelty of carrying her away from all that makes life pleasant and leave her to suffer far more than even a cruel death. Suppose we should be carried off to some distant, dark forest, and left without friend, or food, or shelter. No words could describe our distress and heartache even before hunger came upon us. Let us think of this and remember that home and friends are very dear to kitty also, as the following story clearly shows:

A man had a cat and four kittens he wished to be rid of, so he put them in his wagon one morning when he was going to mill. He dropped them in a lonely wood, eight miles from home, and thought himself well rid of them. He drove four miles further, waited for his grist, and returned late in the afternoon. When three miles from home he saw his cat toiling wearily along with one of her kittens in her mouth. Watching, he soon saw her lay it with the other three in a shady place by the roadside. She was panting and nearly exhausted, but stood over her crying little ones uttering soothing, reassuring little mews, as if to tell them, "Never fear! mother will take care of you and bring you safe home again."

You would think that tabby's tender devotion and love of home must have softened her master's heart so that he could not help putting the whole family in the wagon and taking them back home to a good supper and a soft bed. But this is a true story, so I am compelled to tell you that he drove on leaving these needy creatures to suffer, when they had a right to look to him for help.

The next morning when he opened his door there was the cat, O! so thin and hungry, but with her four treasures safe in their accustomed place.

When you feel like frightening a vagrant cat remember this story and speak kindly to it. And if you are ever tempted to lose a cat or little kitten away from home, think of it. Do not wrong so much devotion, and do not harden your own heart by so cruel a deed. It is far better that a cat should be killed humanely than that it should be driven out to pine and starve, a homeless tramp.

When we have reached the highest civilization, no family will go off for a summer vacation and leave a cat unprovided for. Such a thing is shamefully cruel.

QUESTIONS.

What is the motto of this lesson?
Are kittens usually trained in the things we would have them know and do?
If they fail in good behavior are we often hard upon them?
How does a certain kind man teach his cats to keep off of the table and away from the milk pail?
Might they be taught other points of good manners as well?
Does this man begin his training with kittens or old cats?
Does he make it a point to punish the wrong-doer in the very act?
Why is this?
Does he punish hard?
How does he treat the kitten after punishment?
Why should a kitten be corrected very gently?
Why is a well-fed cat a better mouser than one that is starved?
What food does a cat especially need when she catches many mice?
Are vegetables a good diet for her?

Take notice that she needs little or no meat. She is less liable to fits without it.

Should catnip and grass be supplied, if not within her reach?

Does a cat need water, and should it be clean?

If mice are in the house when is kitty's best time to catch them?

How may her neatness about the house be insured?

Is it cruel to keep a cat by the stove during the day and put her out in the cold at night?

Are cats especially sensitive to cold?

Did you ever know of a cat being taken off to a strange place and left?

How would you like to be purposely lost from home and friends?

Tell the story of the cat and her four kittens.

How many miles did tabby travel to get her four kittens home?

Do you admire such devotion and such home love?

Was that man cruel?

What should he have done, if he could not keep them?

Is it always kinder to kill a cat than to send it adrift?

NOTE TO TEACHER.—Pupils above fifteen should be taught how to kill cats humanely as found at the back of the book, but younger children should be guarded against such knowledge. There is great need that every family should understand how to dispose of cats humanely, and it should be done by *adults*. Emphasize this.

CHAPTER XXVI.
THE DOG.

"The friends thou hast and their affection tried,
Grapple to thee as with hoops of steel."—Shakespeare.

"Where will you find a man always grateful, always affectionate, never selfish, pushing the abnegation of self to the utmost limits of possibility, forgetful of injuries and mindful only of benefits received? Seek him not, it would be a useless task, but take the first dog you meet, and from the moment he adopts you for his master, you will find in him all these qualities. He will love you without calculation. He will find his greatest happiness in being near you; and should you be reduced to beg your bread, not only will he aid you, but he will not abandon you to follow a king to his palace. Your friends may quit you in misfortune, but your dog never; he will die at your feet, or if you depart before him on the great voyage, he will accompany you to your last abode."—*M. Blaze's History of the Dog.*

Spare Hours says: "Every family should have a dog. All can unite upon Rover. He tells no tales, betrays no secrets, never sulks, asks no questions, and is always ready for a bit of fun."

If it is well for every family to have this all-round friend, then no person should fail to study his comfort and welfare.

A fastidious lady said: "Our dog is invaluable for his care of the children, but he smells so bad I can hardly abide him."

The fault was hers. She was very particular about her children's daily baths, but she did not understand that the dog needed a bath or thorough brushing at least once a week to make him a pleasant companion.

Dogs need exercise as do all living things and if kept in the city or in close quarters should be given a good run every day. Sometimes people think it is necessary to keep a dog tied, but this should be avoided if possible. Such confinement will make him cross and dangerous. Let him have his freedom and patiently teach him that its scientific meaning is the right to do as he pleases so long as he does not interfere with the rights of others. A bright dog will learn this and make a good citizen in less time than it takes most boys and girls. He will learn not to bark at the guest that comes and goes in good form, not to hinder any one in the performance of regular duties, not to molest passers on the street, and not to abuse privileges of

house or garden. If, in spite of proper care, he is vicious, he would better be humanely disposed of. All his evil tendencies are aggravated by chaining him, and he becomes a greater menace to general safety than the owner sometimes understands.

It is so easy for even well intentioned people to forget a dog that is confined; and heat, thirst, and the fret of confinement may well drive him into a frenzy. If ever a dog *must* be tied, stretch a wire across the yard or open space affording the widest run possible and let the dog's chain be attached to this by a movable hook or ring, so that he may go back and forth at will.

Be sure your dog has plenty of fresh water. Sometimes he needs more than others, just as you do, according to weather and exercise. Be sure that he is fed twice a day and not overfed nor starved. Don't imagine that meat is the only thing he needs. White bread alone does not count much for his nourishment, but vegetables, especially cabbage and potatoes cooked, are good for him. If he has a tendency to fits, he is much better without meat. He enjoys variety, and for the most part selects his food according to his needs if he has a chance. Sometimes he wants his dog biscuit dry, and again he likes them soaked. Corn bread, brown bread, and oat meal, are wholesome foods for him. Regularity in meals is important. If he has this with plenty of daily exercise and a patch of couch grass within reach (this is his thoroughly reliable medicine chest) and a clean kennel, raised from the ground to avoid the damp, and so arranged as to shelter him from wind and cold; he can hardly fail to be a healthy, happy dog, if he has a few kind words and looks thrown in. Straw and pine shavings make good bedding for the kennel. Be sure it is often changed for health's sake and conscience sake. Be sure, too, that the kennel has thorough ventilation, whether it be a box or a regularly constructed house.

If a horse is put to a high speed on a warm day, he will be wet with sweat. A boy that runs a race in August will perspire at every pore. In either case if a cold draft or a plunge in cold water should suddenly check this perspiration, it would be a very dangerous thing, probably causing death.

A dog perspires only through his tongue. That is the reason he lolls it so much in warm weather and when running. Many do not know this fact, or they would never muzzle their dogs in the summer or on journeys. Not to know, is often very cruel. Dogs may be driven into spasms by being muzzled, so that the heat of the body has not sufficient relief through the perspiration of the tongue.

We are glad to be assured by scientific men, that mad dogs are very rare, much rarer than was once supposed. Right care would make the number even less.

QUESTIONS.

What is the motto of this lesson?
What kind of a friend is the dog?
Will he like you better if you are rich?
Will he desert you if you become very poor?
Are dogs common?
Is it needful then for everybody to understand their rightful care?
Do dogs need to be kept clean, and how?
Do dogs need exercise?
If they are kept in close quarters, how often should they be taken out for a run?
Does confinement tend to make a dog cross?
May almost any dog be taught not to abuse his freedom?
If not, what should be done with him?

If a dog must be tied, how may it be managed so as to give him some freedom?
Does a dog need more water sometimes than others?
Is fresh, clean water important to him?
What food does he require?
Is much meat a necessity for him?
Are there times when he is better without any?
What is his natural medicine?
Look up couch grass.
How often should a dog be fed?
Does he enjoy variety of food?
How should his kennel be arranged for health and comfort?
What is a good bedding?
Does he crave kind words as well as food and shelter?
Where does a horse sweat?
Where does a dog sweat?
Is it hard on him to be muzzled when he is especially heated?
Are there fewer mad dogs than was once supposed?
What would make them fewer still?

CHAPTER XXVII.
THE DOG—(Continued).
"Deeds are better than words."

The dog is not only man's faithful friend but his tireless helper, and he never haggles about wages. He takes the place of the horse in the great snow fields of the Arctic, and who does not know of the splendid rescue party in the Swiss mountains made up of St. Bernard dogs. Their unflinching courage in bitter cold and storm, their intelligence in searching out drift hidden travelers, restoring the exhausted, and bringing other help to those that are beyond their power to help, gives us nobler ideals of life. "The pious monks of St. Bernard" could never have done their gracious work without their dogs. Books upon books have been written and many more might be written, telling of the fidelity, the daring, the subtle intelligence, the unselfish love of dogs. They guard our houses even more securely than the best soldier. The little spaniel proved a safer bodyguard to William of Orange than his picked men. Dogs have laid down their lives to protect a baby in its cradle. They have become outcasts for the sake of an outcast master. They have stayed the hand of burglar and assassin. They have given the fire alarm that in single instances saved hundreds of lives. Their sensitive smell and delicate ear, coupled with their deathless devotion to man, give them at times the character of almost supernatural protectors of him and his.

In herding, driving, and separating cattle and sheep, they far excel the strongest and most willing men. "The Ettric Shepherd" says: "Without the shepherd's dog, the whole of the open mountainous land in England and Scotland would not be worth a sixpence. It would require more hands to manage a flock of sheep, gather them from the hills, force them into houses and folds and drive them to market, than the profits of the whole stock would be capable of maintaining. Well may the shepherd feel an interest in his dog; he it is, indeed, that earns the family's bread, of which he is himself content with the smallest morsel, always grateful, always ready to exert his utmost abilities in his master's interest. Neither hunger, fatigue, nor the worst of treatment will drive him from his side; he will follow him through every hardship, without murmuring or repining, till he literally falls down dead at his feet."

We feel instinctively that there is something noble in a man (however gruff his appearance) that speaks gently to a little child. Who can deny nobility to the dog that not only gives the baby right of way, but stays its toddling steps with tender forethought.

One day, a bold, bad man made his way to the cradle of a baby prince, determined to carry him off, to lose him among poor peasant people, that the crown might fall to another line. The royal baby woke, and looking up with wide wondering eyes, smiled a sweet trusting smile that went straight to the bad man's heart and softened it. He could not wrong the child in the light of that happy smile, and he went away as if led by an invisible hand.

Who can look into a dog's loving human eyes, and lightly treat or wrong so much devotion? With all his wisdom and helpfulness, the dog is yet as dependent on man for the joy of living as the baby upon its mother. Great powerful mastiffs and Newfoundlands that can throw an ox, will hang upon their master's look with almost pathetic self-abnegation. They have no will but to fulfill his will. Many dogs, especially the shepherds, are as sensitive to a frown or harsh word as a tender-hearted child.

If gentleness toward young and tender things bespeaks nobility in a man, surely it cannot mean less in a dog.

Bruno, a powerful dog of all work on an Illinois farm, frequently needed a restraining hand and voice, in his dealings with cattle, horses and hogs, for his zeal for discipline led him into severity, but he was as careful of the babies among the stock as their own mothers. Little chickens could come and steal his breakfast unmolested, but the old hens never dared. One day when an aggressive little brownie with his precocious tail and wings, for some time kept saucily in the way of his next bite, he gathered it up in his capacious mouth and, carrying it several yards, deposited it in the home coop without harming so much as a feather. The cats respected his dignity, but the little kittens played over him at will. Though he did not like it and sometimes whined complainingly, he was even more helpless and defenseless against them than was Mother Tabby herself.

From "Our Home Pets"   Copyright, 1894, by Harper & Brothers

One morning a large flock of sleek white pigs found a hold in the garden fence, which they made haste to scramble through and go exploring. Bruno was called to put them out, but he stood and looked after them, with the indulgent amusement of a foolish mother, that counts the mischief of her very little ones too cute to be corrected. After much urging and threatening, he ran among them and his formidable appearance scared them back to their own side of the fence. But it was a full day before that hole was stopped up, and the pigs kept it hot. They ran in and out almost every hour. They soon learned that Bruno's growls and yelps meant no harm to them, so they pursued their various interests undisturbed by his presence. He was very much attached to the little girl of the house, whose duty it was to keep the pigs out and he delighted to do her bidding; but not even for her sweet sake could he violate this fundamental tenderness of his nature for all young things. She got very tired, chasing from side to side and round and round after twenty pigs, especially when the one she got out came back while she was after another, and she became very stern in her commands to Bruno. Cut to the heart, he would make a wild dash among them, uttering a dismal howl and growl combined, a comical mixture of protest and threat, which the pigs soon came to fear no more than their own contented grunts. Then he turned somersaults among them and performed other heavy gymnastics. The pigs took care that he should not fall upon them, but were otherwise undisturbed. The little mistress could not help laughing in spite of her multiplied task.

" The dog craves food, but he also craves affection. A life higher than his own is needed for his happiness. He looketh at the hand of his master, as the inferior looketh at the superior, when itself is great enough to discover greatness. The dog finds deity in his master. From him he takes law and love both. From him he receives joy so intense that even his master marvels at it, and wonders that so slight a motion of his hand, so brief an utterance from his lips, can make any being so happy. It is because the dog can receive so much, that thought ranks him so high. The capacity of receptiveness gives accurate measurement and gradation to animals and to men.—*Murray*.

QUESTIONS.

What is the motto of this lesson?
Is the dog a faithful servant as well as a faithful friend?
How did they serve in the Alps?
Read up the St. Bernard dogs.
Read up the sledge dogs of the Arctic.
Tell what your dogs can do.
Has much been written about dogs?
Tell about the spaniel of William of Orange.
What special qualities make the dog a man's protector?
In how many different ways he has proven himself able to protect and help man?
What does the Ettric Shepherd say of the service of the shepherd dogs in England and Scotland?
Are shepherd dogs helpful about cattle and other stock?
Do we think well of the rough man that speaks gently to a child?
Are dogs usually careful and kind with children?

If such gentleness makes us like a man, how must it influence us toward a dog?

How did the smile of the baby prince influence the bad man?

Should the loving trust of a dog make us kinder to him?

Are dogs sensitive?

What class of dogs seem most easily hurt by a cross word?

Tell the story of Bruno and the little pigs.

Why didn't he make the pigs go out?

CHAPTER XXVIII.
SHEEP.
"The charm of man is his kindness."—Proverbs.

"Shepherds all, and maidens fair,
Fold your flocks up; the air
Begins to thicken, and the sun
Already his great course hath run.

"Therefore, from all danger lock
Every one his loved flock;
And let your dogs lie loose without,
Lest a wolf come as a scout
From the mountain, and ere day,
Bear lamb or kid away;
Or the crafty, thievish fox,

Break upon your simple flocks.
To secure yourself from these,
Be not too secure in ease;
So shall you good shepherds prove,
And deserve your master's love."
Beaumont and Fletcher.

The following choice bit of description, from Isabel C. Barrows, gives us as clear a picture as an artist's brush:

"Years ago, when some of us whose heads are growing silvery as wool, were young, one of the most picturesque scenes in the course of the year was the sheep washing and shearing. How well we recall a certain pool, filled by a dancing brook that came purling down a hillside in Vermont! Into a fold beside this pool the sheep were driven on a fine June morning, and one by one were caught in strong arms and dipped into the water, where they were well washed. Then they were allowed to dry in a grassy paddock; and, when in the right condition, the sharp shears went snip, snip through the clean, white wool, till the fleece was left in a pile on the grass, and the sheep bounded away, light of heart, to its impatient lamb.

"It all comes back as we recall it—the busy scene—the hurrying shears and swashing waters, the ba-a-ing of the lambs, the scent of the wild strawberries in the air and overhead the bright June sun.

"The wind blew fresh and cool over the New England hills, but there were always sheltered corners where the new-shorn animals could huddle together when they were tired of frisking, or, if a storm came up, they were driven in hot haste to the big barn floor; for the life of a single sheep was of value on these small farms, even if the instinct of kindness had not prompted the owner to protect the dumb creature, whom his own needs had robbed of its warm clothing."

The ease with which sheep glean their food from rocky slopes where tillage is impossible, has made mountainous districts and barren stretches conspicuous for the sheepcotes and feeding flocks. Their helplessness in danger naturally stirs the courage of the shepherd so that many a one has risked his life for the sheep. Legend, tradition, and history, have given us a wealth of anecdotes and stories along this line.

Shepherds must not only be brave and daring, tender and true, but they must be clever and skillful to save the flock and make it thrive. Such work develops heart and head and hand.

At an early day the shepherd's crook was invented to help in climbing, no less than in catching and managing the sheep, and he soon acquired great skill in handling it. So long ago that we can hardly mark the time, the dog was made a helper in this work. His faithfulness, his wisdom and his sympathetic nature made him a most valuable ally. The influence of the life has told on him for good as well as man. The shepherd's collie is everywhere recognized as the most intelligent and devoted breed of dogs.

In some of the towns of Scotland where a bird's-eye view of the flocks was the only thing that made intelligent care of them possible, the shepherd mounted giant stilts, besides which the school boys would appear like grasshoppers.

The hill country of Judea, which is especially a shepherd

land, abounds in pastoral romance and story. There, care and courage were required to protect sheep from the wild beasts of cave and den. In such places one man cannot manage a large number and the good shepherd comes to know every sheep, and they in turn know his voice and answer his call. The life of every sheep and every lamb is precious, and he would brave great danger to rescue and help one. Something akin to family feeling is established between them.

There are beautiful pictures of the shepherd risking his life for the sheep, sheltering the lambkin safe and warm in the front of his smock-frock, scaling a dangerous cliff after some daring climber, carrying the wounded and weary sheep upon his shoulders, or resting upon his crook beside the grazing flock.

In all lands and in all times the shepherd folk have been recognized as a simple, warm-hearted, truth-loving people, whose occupation has ennobled them, helping to quicken the springs of human sympathy without which life is black and barren. Our language and our literature have been greatly enriched with figures and illustrations drawn from this source. The innocent lamb and the timid sheep will mold thought and feeling as long as the old English poets and the Bible are read, even though this intimate care of them should change everywhere, and thus in a measure change man's attitude toward them.

The shepherd has received more than he has given, and this is always true of good service. His occupation has helped him to grow in tender grace and noble wisdom, as well as helped to make him strong and brave. An occupation that can do so much for character is noble and must win respect.

The material benefits sheep lend to us are almost beyond counting. The close, warm flannels that ease the world of shivers; the hose and mittens that shut out aches from toes and fingers; the thick coat, a veritable coat of mail against sharp frost arrows; the fluffy hood and scarf, white and beautiful as fresh drifted snow; the soft, comfortable rug; and the close enfolding blankets between which we are glad to cuddle on a winter's night; these are a few of the blessings which must send a grateful thrill to every heart that comes up to the modest standard of recognizing benefits.

QUESTIONS.

What is the motto of this lesson?
What does the poem say the shepherd should do?
Outline Isabel C. Barrow's picture of the sheep washing and shearing.
What influence does the shepherd's work have upon him?
Look up all you can about the sheep's habit of feeding, and the character of the country where it so frequently gets its living.
Name some of the lands that have long been famous for sheep.
Did the olden shepherd make account of every individual of his flock?
What influence did this have upon him and them?
What developed the strength and courage of the shepherd?
What developed his wisdom and skill?
What developed his sympathies?

What kind of an all-round culture did this give him?

What kind of a character has this given to the shepherd classes?

How has it affected other people?

How long is the influence of the innocent lamb and the timid sheep likely to affect society?

What can you say of an occupation that has such an influence on character?

How many comforts that we receive from sheep can you name?

Who has been the shepherd's great helper?

Are shepherds and sheep frequently mentioned in literature?

Name some of the great authors that have written about sheep and some of the great works of literature in which they figure?

Name some great characters in history that have worked with sheep, and tell something about them.

Name some famous pictures of sheep.

Give some of Shakespeare's shepherds and shepherdesses.

What poem has Milton written about shepherds? (See Lycidus.)

Look up James Hogg, the shepherd poet.

Look up David.

CHAPTER XXIX.

SHEEP—(Continued).

"The humane spirit is the root out of which some of the best flowers of character grow."—Isabel C. Barrows.

" One lesson, shepherd, let us two divide,
Taught both by what God shows and what conceals,
Never to blend our pleasure or our pride
With sorrow of the meanest thing that feels."
Wordsworth.

In the past few years the work of sheep raising has undergone an almost entire transformation in this country. Instead of small companies of scores and hundreds, they are now kept in bands of from two to four thousand on the western plains, herded by a single man with the help of a few collies. There can be little acquaintance with individuals, and many sufferers must go unnoted and die for lack of care. The lambkins that come in cold and windy times, perish in great numbers like early blossoms before the frost. This is one of the sacrifices to the present spirit of doing everything on a large scale. It is significant that the man who cares for sheep in this way is no longer called a shepherd, but a herder. This kind of work does not beautify and ennoble character. "The law of the harvest is to reap more than we sow." When greed of gain brings indifference to loss of life and suffering, it brings with it loss of sympathy and sensibility.

Even New England, which used to be full of pretty

pastoral shepherding, now shows hardly any trace of the old time personal care for the sheep.

The past few years have wrought great changes in their care. Over two-thirds of the wool is sold without washing, and therefore it is called for much earlier than used to be the custom so as to get it off before it takes on its spring

dirt. Hence, the sheep are shorn sometimes the first of April, and then left to face the spring storms unsheltered. Very many of them die, and all suffer as we would at such time in summer clothes.

The artist, Enneking, who went out into the rural districts two successive seasons to catch a picturesque sheep-washing scene for his canvas, such as described in the preceding chapter, found himself a second time too late. Falling in with some of the woolgrowers on a Sunday he drew from them a full story of existing conditions, for they mistook him for a wool agent. They told how the early shearing made them lose, in some cases, half the sheep in the late, cold storms, and how sometimes the poor, little lambs were frozen in the fields. They wound up by demanding a higher price for the wool to make up for such heavy losses.

The artist preached them a sermon worthy of the day, telling them to save their missionary money and get some one to teach them their duty to the dumb animals. Adding, that it was the essence of heathenism not to care for the brute that could not care for itself.

It is cruel to take off a sheep's warm overcoat in the cold springtime, and leave it unprotected.

If chilling changes come unexpectedly after shearing, the sheep should be given a warm shelter. Unless they can be protected in the time of need, no man has a right to keep them.

Every sheep needs more or less personal supervision to prevent the breeding of diseases and the accumulation of pests. Such attention cannot be given by a single man to four thousand sheep. Where the rainy season is long continued they need protection from the wet, as from the cold in other climates.

"The law of the harvest is to reap more than we sow."

Besides the steady, sure profits which come from the intelligent, kindly care of these timid, trustful creatures, there is the discipline and refinement of feeling which comes to man as one of the best fruits of life. Cruelty to a defenseless animal makes the person practicing it so much less manly. "The humane spirit is the root out of which some of the best flowers of character grow."

QUESTIONS.

What is the motto of this lesson?
Commit Wordsworth's lines.
What are the changes in sheep raising in the past few years?
Where are these large herds mostly kept?
Why is the keeping of large bands by a single man neither kind nor economic?
What is the law of the harvest?
Is this true of weeds as well as grain?
What are the present conditions of sheep raising in New England?
Why is the cold hard on sheep after they are sheared?
Should they be sheltered if it turns cold and stormy after shearing?
Do sheep need protection from continued wet weather?
Tell the story of the artist Enneking.
Why did he so severely denounce those farmers?
What effect does cruelty have upon one who practices it?
What effect does kindness to dumb animals have upon character?
Does the right care of sheep seem to be especially refining?

CHAPTER XXX.

THE HOG.

The noble and unselfish mind makes better and happier every life it touches.

The common phrase, "dirty as a pig pen," is a reproach to the master rather than to the hog, for this animal keeps its nest cleaner than almost any other quadruped. Even in a close sty, so long as there is any possibility, it keeps a dry, clean bed. True, it will lie down in muddy pools, but this is to cool itself, and shows its relation to the hippopotamus and rhinoceros. The hog in a native state dwells in the merry green-wood, picking up nuts and digging roots for a living, and leads a care-free, happy life. Domestication has greatly changed him. Wild he has comparatively long legs and a slim body, and requires from three to four years for development. To-day. the accepted hog of the farmer is grown in a year and has a large heavy body and short legs. But in spite of these changes he still delights in fresh fields and pastures green. With the closer settlement of the country, and the breaking up of large holdings into small ones, his confinement has become closer, and with all this crowding there has been small care on the part of the master to keep the sty clean. While piggy has lived, and *seemed to thrive* in this way, perfectly healthy hogs are few, and great numbers die of disease every year.

There is a popular idea that the pig is very gross and stupid, which is really at the bottom of much of his neglect and abuse. Prof. N. S. Shaler says: "The hog is the only animal that has been degraded by contact with man." This is a severe charge. The noble, unselfish mind makes happier and better every life it touches.

This same professor ranks the hog highest of our domestic mammalia in intelligence. See page 143, "Domesticated Animals." He tells of seeing a plain pig in Virginia that could pick out the cards bearing its own age, the name of Lincoln, and other great men, and make small mathematical calculations at the request of its master. It performed these tasks somewhat after the manner of a lazy school boy, but it certainly comprehended what it did.

The following story clearly illustrates the reasoning faculty of this much abused, much slandered creature. The incident happened at an early day in Indiana. A certain rail fence dividing a wood and a cornfield, had a large hollow log for the foundation of one of its panels. The log was somewhat crooked so that one end opened into the inviting cornfield, and the other end opened into the oak and beach wood pasture, where a number of hogs fed sumptuously upon dropping nuts and acorns. But one hog, at least, looked upon the alluring corn and was tempted. If, with set purpose, she went searching for an entrance to the field, we know not, but true it is one day she found the hollow log and perceived in it the desired opening; with some difficulty, it may be imagined, she made the passage, and that Eutopean adage, "a pig in clover," lost its meaning in the higher delights this cornfield afforded. The master chanced to discover the marauder and put her out with haste and much trouble, having to throw down the fence to make a way. After walking the entire line of dividing fence, he was greatly puzzled to understand how the miscreant got through. And the puzzle grew and grew when she returned to this favorite feeding ground day after day. More careful search was made, and, at last tracks at both ends of the log, and bristles left upon its inner walls, disclosed the secret passage. The farmer so adjusted it that both ends opened into the pasture and kept watch to see what might happen. Soon came the corn-loving hog, and noting nothing new, made her laborious way through the log, struggling and grunting, and, in a particularly tight place, squealing softly. It was with a great grunt of satisfaction she came out upon the ground. This was quickly followed by a grunt of anxious inquiry, and then a whole row of exclamation. The fence was still between her and El Dorado. With evident feeling of injury she went back to the other end and started through again with great determination. The passage seemed even more difficult the second time than it was the first. With much complaint and scolding she at last made her way out again. Finding herself still shut out from her heart's desire, she gave one great despairing and frightened grunt and ran into the woods. As far as is known she never returned to that spot again. Like people she was scared at what she did not understand. She certainly showed a reasoning power that entitles her to be called intelligent. To conclude that the log as she first found it would take her into the cornfield was a real exercise of reason. To run away from the unknown and unknowable is not unlike crude humanity.

If every one who keeps a pig would second its efforts to be neat, would give it sufficient room and shelter from the storms, would look carefully to the cleaning and drainage of the sty, would see to it that the pig had the freedom of some grass plot, now and then, or at least had green feed thrown it, would insist on the cleanliness of its food and drink, avoiding distillery and brewery slops, and other putrid food, would be free with kindly words and pats, as one good man has said, "No doubt the breed of hogs would be improved a hundred per cent. in a few years."

Some progressive growers of this animal now give them the daily freedom of a pea field or clover field, and find it pays well.

The young of many wild animals are unattractive, not to say ugly. Many birds that are remarkable for grace and beauty have clumsy, naked baby birds that can be pretty only in their fond mother's eyes; but the young of our domestic animals are irresistibly winsome and beautiful, as a rule, and the baby pig is no exception. Shapely, active, knowing, affectionate, and clean, they captivate any unprejudiced observer.

Compte says, "The animals about us become partakers of our humanity." Let us look to it that we do not make them partakers of our degradation. "The noble and unselfish mind makes better and happier every living life it touches."

QUESTIONS.

What is the motto of this lesson?

Does the phrase "dirty as a pig pen" reflect on man?

Does the hog show that it likes to be neat, even above other animals?

How does the hog live in a native state?

What are the great changes that have come to it in domestication?

What is the popular opinion of the hog?

What influence has that had upon animal and master?

What does Prof. N. S. Shaler say about the intelligence of the hog?

What does he tell of a trained pig?

Tell the story of the hog that got into the corn field.

How did it manifest reason?

What are some of the important changes that should be made in the care of hogs?

If everybody that keeps a hog would make these improvements in its care, what would be likely to result?

Is there a tendency among progressive farmers to-day to restore the primitive conditions of the hog?

What does Compte say about animals?

Shall we make them sharers of our good or evil?

What of the young of many wild animals?

What of the uniform beauty of the young of domestic animals?

What of the attractiveness of the little pig?

Make a study of baby pigs and compare notes.

CHAPTER XXXI.

THE COW.

"He who serves well and speaks not, merits more
Than they who clamor loudest at the door."—Longfellow.

Our animal friends do many things for us that we can't do for ourselves. Whatever we do for them is bread cast upon the waters to return to us often times in few days. Or it is like good seed sown on fertile ground, yielding us a hundred fold.

"Man is very clever—there is no doubt about that. He can do many wonderful things. He can talk by means of a telegraph wire with people at the other end of the world. Through a telephone he can make his voice heard hundreds of miles. By means of his potter's wheel he can make the very clay into endless beautiful and useful shapes, dainty vases and graceful pitchers.

"But this one thing a man can't do, no, not the wisest that ever lived; he can't change a handful of grass into a cup of milk. This great work has been given to a humble creature, the cow. She is lent to be man's servant, is trusted to him, and she can do this thing which is beyond the master's power. Should not the master treat this unselfish, mild, and gentle servant with every care?"—*Edith Carrington, from "Workers Without Wage."*

Milk, butter, and cheese are among the first necessities of the civilized world. If every family does not own a cow, almost every family uses one or more of the cow's products, It is simple justice that we should make these

creatures comfortable and happy that do so much for us.
Upon their happiness and comfort depend the wholesomeness of their milk, butter, and cheese; therefore our own welfare is bound up in theirs.

If it is never our pleasant task to put some gentle bossie to pasture or fill the pail with foaming milk, still, *how* it is done is much to us if we use dairy products; our health and life even depend upon it. So every one should make a study of the care of cows.

These mild-eyed creatures show such sweet content, such gentle gratitude for every good that comes to them, that they have become the artist's ideal of peaceful beauty. Many of the great pictures that men and women crowd to see are cattle scenes. But we do not need to visit art galleries for visions of pastoral peace. He who walks through the fields on a summer day and opens the eyes of his soul, may see sleek heifers, white and red and spotted, crop the fragrant clover or cool themselves in some clear pool, making a picture lovelier and more restful than brush or pencil have ever caught.

Rosa Bonheur has made the world better by her celebrated paintings of the ox and the winsome calf. Love for animals has opened up this great field of art to her. Kindness for any creature will make love for it, and love is a magic glass reflecting beauty. The more we catch the beauty of life in field and wood, the better we shall be.

Sometimes cows are called stupid, but they show a tender mother love and a sense of gratitude that in man would be called virtue.

George T. Angell, the great friend of animals, gives us this bit of experience:

One day when he was crossing Boston Common, he found a cow sadly tangled in her long tether. She had struggled to free herself until she was exhausted, all the

while becoming more hopelessly tied up. He cut the rope and got her on her feet, then brought her some water —it was a hot day—and she drank eagerly. She then rubbed her head against his arm and mooed softly. A bright girl who took an old man's seat in a crowded car one day, forgot to thank her benefactor. But this cow did not omit that courtesy! When Mr. Angell reached home, he told his friends that he had relieved a lady in distress and she rewarded him with a kiss.

QUESTIONS.

What is the motto of this lesson?
What does it mean?
What are some of the wonderful things that man can do?
Can he make milk from grass?
What animal makes milk most abundantly?
What return should we make to the cow for her service to us?
What are some of the products of the cow that are of great importance to civilized man?
What should we do for the cow in return for her benefits?
Does our own safety depend in any way upon her kindly treatment?
Do most families use one or more dairy products?
Does this make it worth while for every one to learn how cows should be treated?
Why is it important for you to study these things if you do not expect to take care of a cow?
What great artist has painted cattle scenes?
Read up Rosa Bonheur.
Might almost any one in a half day's walk see beautiful pastoral scenes if their inward eyes were open to it?
What helps us to see the beauty in men and animals?
Do cows show strong mother love? Give examples of it.
Do they ever show gratitude?
Tell Geo. T. Angell's story.

CHAPTER XXXII.
THE CARE OF THE COW.
"He who is not actively kind, is cruel."—Ruskin.

One cow that is in good condition, well fed, and kept in a warm barn, will yield as much milk as two cows that are insufficiently fed and are stalled in a cold, dark, damp place. One thing most essential to the owner is the health of the cow.

It is at all times both humane and good judgment to compare the conditions of the creatures of the animal kingdom to the physical conditions of the human family. Man well fed, well housed, and healthy, is capable of performing a great amount of work. Man ill fed, badly housed, and sickly, can do but little.

The patient cow may be likened to a living machine (formed to do special work). Her special work is the production of milk, and that production is regulated by the amount and suitability of the food she receives, and the care and condition of her home.

This being true, it pays in dollars and cents, to treat her well. In winter she is especially dependent on her owner for proper food and shelter. She should be kept clean and dry and at night should be given dry bedding. The floor of her stall should be raised at least four inches above the surrounding floor for drainage, and it should be nearly level. Many a cow is strained and becomes muscle sore, on account of the uneven floor on which she is forced to stand. The constant changing of the weight of the body from one foot to another in order to get into a restful position, causes much distress. It is a great comfort to the cow to be able to lick herself. Whenever it is practicable, she should be so tied that she can lick any part of her body. Behind the cow, for an absorbent, there should be dry earth, sawdust, plaster, or peat.

The barn should be well ventilated, light and air coming from behind the animal. Windows should be arranged in the south and east sides of the barn to let in plenty of sunlight. The temperature should at all times be kept above freezing, and if this cannot be done, it is best to blanket the cattle. When the weather is pleasant, turn the cows out for exercise, but be sure to stable them before the temperature begins to lower in the afternoon. It is better they should stand in the barn on cold and stormy days, for when they become wet much of the warmth of the body must be exhausted to dry the thick coat of hair, and besides there is danger of severe cold, which may produce tuberculosis.

A thorough brushing every day adds to the cow's comfort and content, removing liability to disease as well. A stiff broom corn brush is good for this purpose.

It is important that a cow be kept quiet and be treated with the utmost gentleness. She has a very nervous organization and should on no account be frightened. Remember, no blows! No kicks! No stones! No loud words! These distress and disturb her and will lessen the flow and injure the quality of the milk. Kindness to domestic animals is capital well invested.

If possible, the same person should always milk. Let it be one who is naturally kind, who inspires the cow with confidence, so that if she moves or puts the milker to inconvenience, she will not expect punishment.

It is well to feed a cow so that she will be through eating before milking begins, then she will stand quietly and give her whole attention to the operation.

It is important that the milker be clean in person and that the stall be kept very clean. There should be no dust flying and the udder should be thoroughly brushed or wiped before milking. Remove the milk from the barn before it has time to cool and absorb any bad odor or flavor.

No rule can be given that can apply to all cows, but it is true economy to give a cow plenty of good, wholesome food. The feeding should be based on the law that the desired product results from the food. Avoid brewer's slops and grains; if used, after a time the cow's teeth will blacken and decay, and the milk will be thin and blue, the butter white and tasteless. Roots should be fed, as they aid in keeping the digestive organs in a healthy condition and increase the flow of milk. Have salt where a cow can get as much as she wants. Rock salt is the best. It acts as a tonic and corrective.

Give a cow all the fresh water she wants, and in winter the chill should be taken off. The late Honorable E. F. Bowditch found that by giving twenty cows water at a temperature of ninety-two degrees, the supply of milk was increased two hundred quarts per week, conclusively proving the value of warm drinks over cold.

A cow should never be allowed to drink stagnant or impure water. It produces fever and ropy milk. Samples of milk from cows that have been drinking from stagnant pools, show swarms of animal life exactly the same as those found in the water. Such milk is unfit for food and produces disease and death.

In New York it is a misdemeanor, punishable by fine and imprisonment, to keep milk cows in crowded or unhealthy places, or to feed them with distillery waste (usually called swill) or any other substance in a state of putrefaction or fermentation. Tuberculosis is frequently found in cows so fed.

Have regular hours for feeding, milking, and grooming. Food should be clean. It is better to stack hay out of doors than to store it over a barn cellar containing manure. The hay is permeated with the fumes rising from the manure, which carry germs of disease; such hay is unfit for the cow. Hens should never be allowed in the barn, or about the hay. Keep the manger clear of any refuse that the cow declines to eat.

The little calf should be kept dry, in warm, clean quarters, where its mother can see it, and for the first month fed on warm milk, then a spoonful of shorts may be added, gradually increasing the amount and adding other grains if desired. While no feed is too good for a calf, or any growing animal, yet over-feeding young heifers is likely to lessen their value as milkers. The mother of a very young calf should on no account be given cold water to drink.

Fright or cruel usage may render a cow's milk absolutely poison. A celebrated dairyman says he always speaks as kindly to a cow as he would to a lady, and he requires like gentleness and kindness from his helpers.

We cannot treat unkindly any of God's creatures that supply us with food, without danger of suffering ourselves.

Cows learn to know their names, and come when called. Many a young girl has had a petted heifer, that wore a ribbon and rejoiced in her mistress' affection as did the beautiful " Zephyr of Evangeline."

" The great American statesman and orator, Daniel Webster, asked, just before he died, that all his cattle, which he loved so much, should be driven past his window, that he might see them for the last time. As they came, one by one, he called them each by name, and was soothed and comforted by their answered looks of intelligent affection."—*George T. Angell.*

The love of these dumb things is very sweet to human hearts.

QUESTIONS.

What is the motto of this lesson?
What does it mean?
What is the advantage of a cow *well kept* over one poorly kept?
What is the most essential thing to the owner of stock?
How do poor conditions and poor food affect man?
Does this teach us what kind of care animals need?
What is the special business of the cow?
On what does the amount and quantity of her milk depend?
Does it pay in dollars and cents to treat her well?
In winter is she especially dependent upon her owner for food and comfort?
Is it important that she be kept dry?
What about bedding?
What are the two important points to be observed in the floor of her stall?
What injury results from an uneven floor?

Should a cow be tied so that she may lick herself?
What are good absorbents?
What is the cheapest absorbent in your locality?
What about the ventilation of the barn?
Where should the windows be?
What about the temperature of the barn?
Do cows need exercise?
What time should be chosen for this and what should be avoided?
What disease may be produced by colds?
What makes a good brush for grooming?
Is quiet important to the well-being of a cow?
Is she a nervous animal?
What effect does unkindness have on the flow and quality of the milk?
What kind of a person should do the milking?
Is it better that the same person should milk day after day?
When is it best to feed?
Is cleanliness important and why?
Is it important that the milk be quickly removed from the barn? If so, why?
What is the law of true feeding?
What will happen if brewers' slops and grains are fed?
Are roots valuable food?
How should salt be given?
What of watering?
What did the Hon. E. F. Bowditch prove?
What is the effect of stagnant water on the cow and on her milk?
What does a microscope show in such milk?

How does the New York law protect people from the evils resulting from bad feeding?

Is regularity of feeding, milking, and grooming important?

Does cleanliness of food count for anything with cattle?

Is it well to have hens laying in the haymow or manger?

Is it well to allow anything of refuse to accumulate in the manger?

How should the little calf be kept and how should it be fed?

Should cold water be given the mother of a very young calf?

What does a celebrated dairyman say is his way of speaking to his cows?

Do fright and suffering poison a cow's milk?

Have calves often been pets?

Do cattle learn their names?

What of Daniel Webster and his cattle?

Is the affection of these dumb creatures a pleasant thing?

CHAPTER XXXIII.

THE HORSE.

Truth is Power and Kindness is Grace. He that stands first in these is King of his Age.

Henry Ward Beecher says: "Society owes the horse a debt of gratitude. He has ministered to progress; has made social intercourse possible where otherwise it would have been slow, or altogether impossible. He has virtually extended the strength of man, augmented his speed, doubled his time, decreased his burdens, released him from drudgery, and helped to make him free.

"For eminent moral reasons the horse deserves to be

bred, trained, and cared for with scrupulous care. Teaching men how to do it has been left too long to those who look upon the horse as an instrument of gambling gains or mere physical pleasure."

A fine edged tool is a great help and safeguard in skillful hands, but in awkward, careless hands is a constant menace and destruction. So it is with the strong, sensitive horse. With a wise and gentle master he is docile and trusty almost beyond belief. But with a harsh, ignorant, or cruel master, he often becomes a terrible destroyer of life and property. The safety of an engine depends upon the engineer. The safety of a horse depends upon the driver.

With almost human sensibility and intelligence the horse responds to his master's guidance and affection, as friend responds to friend.

"Much is said about good temper in horses. Much more needs be said about good temper in drivers. The truth is, we must govern ourselves before we can hope to govern the lower animals. A man or a boy flushed with passion, his brain charged with heated blood, and eyes blazing with rage, is not in a condition to think clearly; and it is just this thinking clearly that is, above all else, needed in directing and controlling horses. Hence it is that contact with horses, and an actual experience in teaching them, are two of the finest disciplines a person can have."—*W. H. H. Murray, in the " Perfect Horse."*

The hearing of the horse is very acute. Fifteen vibrations per second produce the lowest sound audible to the human ear, but the horse easily catches the sound from ten. The war horse that "scents the battle from afar" is not a poetic myth but a fact of history. He both hears and smells with marvelous acuteness.

He is not satisfied without a three-fold examination of everything out of the ordinary that comes in his way; that is, he must see, smell, and touch an awesome log or umbrella, etc., before he is quite sure it may be harmless. He seems to rely on sight least of all and on touch, perhaps, most; for Rary thinks it is not for the sake of smelling alone that he likes to get his nose against everything. It is his most sensitive organ of touch. It is more sensitive even than human lips, which physiologists tell us are the most delicately tactile portion of the human body. This helps us to understand the great cruelty of striking a horse on the nose. Indeed, striking him anywhere seems like a brutal and cowardly thing in most cases, his organism is so highly nervous and sensitive. " Brains are almost always better than whips."

" Almost every wrong act of a horse is caused by fear, excitement, or mismanagement. One harsh word will increase the pulse of a nervous horse ten beats per minute.
* * *

" In stabling a colt for the first time quietly walk around him and let him go in of his own accord. * * * Do not undertake to drive him, but give him a little less room outside by gently closing in around him. Do not raise your arms, but let them hang at your side, for you might as well raise a club. The horse has never studied anatomy, and does not know but they may unhinge themselves and fly at him.

" Always use a leather halter and be sure it does not draw tight about his nose if he pulls on it. * * * *

" It is just as natural for a horse to try to get his head out of anything that hurts or feels unpleasant, as it is for you to get your hand out of the fire. The cords of a rope halter are hard and cutting; this makes him raise his head and draw on it; as soon as he pulls, the slip noose tightens and pinches his nose, then he will struggle for life, perchance, throw himself. But this is not the worst.. A horse that has once pulled on his halter can never be as well trained as one that has never pulled at all. * * *

" A colt's nature must be studied that his movements may be understood. We might naturally suppose, from the horse applying his nose to everything new to him, that he always does so for the purpose of smelling these objects; but I believe that it is as much for the purpose of feeling, and that he makes use of his nose as we do of our hand, because it is the only organ by which he can feel with much delicacy.

" Young horses, when first brought to a large town, where they must meet many strange objects, if judiciously treated, not flogged and illused, lose their fears without losing their courage."—*Rary.*

Col. Greenwood says: "The great thing in horsemanship is to get the horse to be of your party; not only get him to obey, but get him to obey willingly."

We do not understand his language very well and he does not wholly understand ours, though Prof. Bristol's school of horses would seem to prove that the mathematical pony, Sultan, and the tiny mule, Dynamite, understood their master's every word; but he was confined to a limited vocabulary, and the form of his commands were never varied. So after all it is not strange that misunderstandings should arise between men and horses with so limited a medium for exchange of ideas.

As the children came trooping into a certain ward school, one morning, the teacher noticed a strange boy among them. She bade him to come to her, but he did not mind. Stepping down the aisle she laid her hand upon his head and looked kindly into his big blue eyes. He smiled brightly and spoke in Swedish. He could not understand a word of English. She gave him a place at her desk, set him copies and practiced him on the most common words and phrases at every odd moment. He would try a hundred times on a hard word if she asked him to, so that he was soon able to do work in class. One day when she praised his progress he said eagerly, his beautiful eyes shining with love: "Your goodness makes things easy to me."

What if she had punished him when he could not understand her? That would have been wicked and foolish. It is equally wicked and foolish to punish a horse because he does not understand. Surely brains and hearts are better than whips.

There are many beautiful stories of the Arabs and their steeds which hardly exaggerate the swiftness of the latter or their devotion to their masters. The tale of Sheik Ilderim and his four colts living in the same tent, is no fancy sketch. The horsemen of the desert treat their colts almost like children, accustoming them to caress and control almost from the beginning; and their horses are the most docile in the world, delighting to do their master's bidding, proud to carry him fleet and far. But these same docile horses become unfaithful and dangerous under harsh treatment.

Ludden's Horse Book makes this clear statement: "The bodily feelings which a human being experiences under any circumstances are similar to those felt by the horse under like circumstances. So a simple rule for our guidance is afforded by the conclusion that what would be painful and disagreeable to us will be just the same to them."

Not only those who feed and groom horses should understand their proper care; every one who rides or drives and every one who cares to lessen the sum of wrong and pain should study it. A gentle word from a kindly woman has loosened a tight check rein, the persuasion of a small boy has put aside the cruel whip, and the wheel blocked by a ready girl has saved an overstrain to many a good horse.

Since the rapid development of electricity as a motor power and the extensive adoption of the bicycle as a means of locomotion the horse is spared many burdens and hardships. But at the same time he has lost an important place in business and pleasure and has fallen into neglect that is something like the displacement of a favorite at court. Kind hearts should use redoubled vigilance in his behalf these days. George T. Angell makes this request to every boy and girl, and I would pass it on to every man and woman:

" When you see a miserable looking horse on the street, one you really pity, say in the kindest tones, ' I pity that horse.' "

That horse will be better taken care of very soon, for no man will care to drive many days through the streets of a city where people are ready to tell him every time he stops, that they pity his horse,

"To His Horse."—By Bayard Taylor.

"Come, my beauty! Come, my desert darling!
  On my shoulder lay thy glossy head!
Fear not, though the barley sack be empty,
  Here's the half of Hassan's scanty bread.

Thou shalt have thy share of dates, my beauty!
  And thou knowest my water-skin is free;
Drink and welcome, for the wells are distant,
  And my strength and safety lie in thee.

Bend thy forehead now, to take my kisses!
  Lift in love thy dark and splendid eye;
Thou'rt glad when Hassan mounts the saddle,—
  Thou'rt proud he owns thee, so am I."

QUESTIONS.

How has the horse earned our gratitude, in Henry Ward Beecher's judgment?

Is a fine edged tool a good thing in skillful hands?

Is it a safe thing in awkward, careless hands?

Is the sensitiveness of the horse an advantage if he is rightly used?

On whom does the safety of an engine depend?

On whom does the safety of a horse depend?

What does a good driver need more than strength?

Can any man match strength with a fine horse?

Has the horse more acute hearing than man?

Are all of his senses acute?

Which does he seem to make most of in examining strange objects?

Why is it especially cruel to strike a horse on the nose?

What is the safest, kindest thing to do for a frightened horse?

Is it helpful to whip him past a post or umbrella that frightens him?

In what ways are "brains better than whips?"

Why is it easy for misunderstandings to arise between men and horses?

Look up "the intelligence of the horse," and find out what you can about Prof. Bristol's School of Horses.

Tell the story of the Swede boy and his teacher.

Does kindness make things easy for animals?

Are love and patience better than whips in discipline?

What does Murray say about a horseman's need of self-control?

What does Rary say about training a colt?

What does Greenway say about the importance of winning a horse to be of your party?

In what ways may those of us who do not handle horses lighten their burdens and relieve their sufferings?

What does George T. Angell ask of every boy and girl?

Look up the Arab horse, and the love his master bears him.

Look up Sheik Ilderim and his colts in "Ben Hur."

Why are the Arab horses so docile?

Why do they become vicious sometimes?

Commit Bayard Taylor's poem "To His Horse."

What proofs can you give that "truth is power and kindness is grace?"

How may he that stands first in these things be truly said to be king of his age?

Do mind and heart rule to-day as never before?

Should truth and goodness of right hold sway?

Are they gaining power to-day, and shall you and I help them on?

CHAPTER XXXIV.

THE CARE OF THE HORSE.

Kindness is the Midas-Touch that Changes all to Gold.

" Without a pinion winged thou art,
And fleetest with thy load;
Bridled art thou without a rein,
And spurred without a goad."

Bayard Taylor.

Mr. Rary, who tamed Cruiser, the most vicious stallion in all England, in three hours, who accustomed wild colts to the halter with hardly an effort, who held great audiences spellbound while he talked on horse training, says that kindness was his only secret.

"Power is put into the locomotive by fuel, into the horse by food. Neither can supply one particle more power than is thus furnished them, and it would be no more foolish to whip an engine for lack of strength than to whip a horse for that reason. But in the latter case it is more than foolish; it is wicked. Overwork, scant food, neglect, and abuse are costly mistakes, and have reduced the average life of a horse from thirty to fifteen years, incurring an annual loss of fifty millions of dollars in this country alone. Add to this losses from illness, lameness, and accident, due to the same cause, and you get the economic waste of cruelty to horses.

The smallness of the horse's stomach is in itself sufficient evidence that it was designed for a frequent feeder. [See the cut on opposite page from Mayhew in "Golden Rules for Animals."] He does not ruminate as the ox, and therefore must eat more slowly, and must have more concentrated food. Vegetables make a good variety for him, especially when fresh grass cannot be had.

To cut down feed because oats are high is expensive economy.

The Arabs are as careful to have clean food for their horses as for themselves. In that they are both wise and kind. The horse's acute sense of smell makes a sour

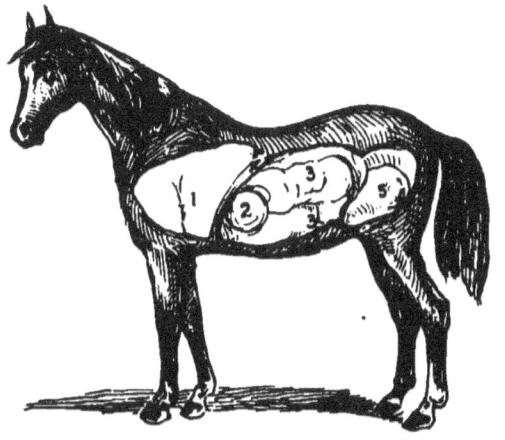

1, the lungs; 2, the stomach; 3, the colon; 4, the diaphragm; 5, situation of the bladder.

manger, dusty hay, dirty corn or oats, and impure water, very offensive to him. But in spite of this fact he will drink from a muddy pool or stream in preference to drinking hard water, though clean, so much does he prefer soft water.

Fresh water from a clean vessel should be given a horse three times a day. Never drive or work a horse immediately after a heavy drink or feed. Never give him cold water when he is hot and tired. A little warm water will rest and refresh him, but he must not be allowed to drink too much at such a time. A quart or two from a pool or spring as he journeys will not harm him. Warming ice water inside of any stock is always costly. Water before feeding.

Irregular salting is bad for any animal, and it is especially bad for the horse. If unaccustomed to it he is likely to eat greedily, and this produces great thirst. If at such a time he is allowed to drink all the cold water he wants, death will most probably be the result. Prepare him for a constant supply by giving a half teaspoonful every day for a week, after which a brick of dairy salt may be kept before him all the time. It will prevent colic and bots.

Regularity of food and drink are important to him as to most animals.

Being a good chewer, unground grains are better for the horse than shorts and meal, inducing a better flow of saliva, which helps his digestion. Rye in any form is injurious to many horses. Bran may be fed to advantage once or twice a day, especially in the shedding season. If work horses are put on night pasture their grain rations should not be shortened. They need both. Horses unaccustomed to green feed should be given it gradually; otherwise it may give them the colic. Green feed makes them thrive.

The best hay is cheapest and should be kept clean.

A horse should be well groomed every day. For this work no instrument equals a good stiff broom, with the handle cut down to a convenient length. Don't use the currycomb about the head, and see that it is not too sharp when used on other parts. In the shedding season an old, well-worn comb is the best thing.

If the fetlocks are frozen or dried with mud they are put in shape for easy cleaning with a little warm water, then rapid rubbing with an old burlap does the work. They are a protection from wind and cold and should never be cut.

Clean your horse outside the stable, if possible, for the dust fouls his manger and makes him loathe his food.

A foul stable is sickening to man and beast; it should be thoroughly cleaned every day. Damp floors soften the hoofs and produce scratches. Use plenty of plaster or other absorbent to absorb the ammonia and moisture. Look out for good ventilation and prevent draughts.

Plenty of light is important in stables for the same reasons that plenty of light is important in houses. Pure air is also essential for the healthy lungs of the horse and consequently for the health of his whole body.

The reflection of light from snow is as hard on a horse's eyes as on a man's and may produce blindness if the transition from a dark stable to the bright glare is sudden.

Next to straw, sawdust is the cleanest, sweetest, and most economical bedding for a stall. Tanbark and sawdust mixed, are good. Many a horse stands up all night because he has not comfortable quarters in which to lie down. An even floor is essential. He would rather stand with his head down hill than up. If the floor slopes back for drainage let the bedding be thinner in front that he may have a level surface to stand upon.

A horse loose in a box-stall is safer and more comfortable than if tied. But if he must be fastened the halter should be just long enough for him to rest his head on the floor; otherwise he may become entangled and killed. Valuable horses have been lost by too much halter and the excuse "I did not know," could not mend matters then.

Gentle tones and movements about a stable contribute much to the comfort and welfare of the occupants. A horse appreciates a musical voice with kind intonations. To get horses out of a burning building throw the harness on them, if at hand. It gives them a sense of something ordinary. Put a blanket or anything that may be caught up, over their heads and lead them gently so as to inspire confidence.

Frosty bits take the skin off of a horse's mouth like a severe burn. Carry the bridles with you to the house when you go to breakfast and put them near the stove; or hold the bits in your hands and warm them with your breath, or dip them in cold water. Find some way of getting the frost out on a cold morning.

No one kind of bit can be recommended for every horse, but a small wire bit is always cruel and so is any bit that cuts the mouth; that goes without saying. Take care of a horse's mouth. His comfort and your safety depend upon it. A callous mouth is no more sensitive than a callous hand, and on the sensitiveness of the horse's mouth depends his quick response to the rein.

Be as careful about the fit of a harness as of the fit of a coat or gown. A collar that galls the shoulders is an inexcusable cruelty. Look to it that the hames are not drawn so close as to pinch the neck. See that none of the straps are too tight.

The check-rein lessens pulling power, irritates nerves, makes bad tempers, creates diseases, and shortens life. Naturally the head is lowered in pulling up hill; try it yourself. Veterinary surgeons, horse trainers, and humane observers unite in denouncing the tight check-rein as a wanton, wicked cruelty, without excuse or palliation. It has caused many a disaster and who can measure the pain it has cost the much-enduring horse.

In Russia blinders are never used and a shying horse is hardly known. A blind bridle prevents a horse from distinctly seeing anything behind or at the side, and a shadowy glimpse may be full of terrors when a full view would be reassuring. In Russia blinders are unknown and a shying horse is scarcely heard of. Experts say that this foolish fashion has ruined many a horse's eyes. It puts them on a strain. When the world fully understands that "truth is power and kindness is grace" no such instruments of torture as the blinder and the check-rein will have leave or license from society for the kings and queens of the age, who give social law, will be first in love and mercy.

Horse Maxims.

Make haste slowly for the first mile when starting out for a long drive and slow up again toward the end. Go slowly down hill and give frequent rests on a long, steep climb. A good brake on a wagon may save years to a horse.

Remember that "Kindness is the Midas-touch that changes all to gold." If your resources are small, your work heavy and your time short, still intelligent kindness will enable you to find some way of making every creature in your care happy and comfortable. Have a quick ear and a sympathetic heart for these helpers that never haggle about prices, but give their all and receive gratefully whatever kindly care we bestow upon them.

Questions.

What is the motto of this lesson?
What was Rary's secret of success?
How do the locomotive and the horse get power?
Would a sane man whip a locomotive for lack of power?
Is it wicked as well as weak to whip a horse for such lack?
What are some costly mistakes in the management of horses?
What is the average yearly cost of cruelty to horses in this country?
Are variety and regularity of food important for horses?
What does the small size of a horse's stomach indicate?
Does the horse ruminate?
What difference does this make in his manner of feeding and kind of food?

What may take the place of fresh grass?
Does it pay to cut down feed because it is high priced?
Why is clean food so important to the horse?
Why are unground grains better than ground for him?
Is rye a safe feed for all horses?
When is bran feed most useful?

Should the rations of working horses be diminished because they are on night pasture?

Why should horses be accustomed to green feed gradually?

Does a horse like hard water?
Is it well to work a horse soon after a heavy feed or drink?
What of cold water when a horse is heated?

Is it a good thing for a horse to have a constant or regular supply of salt?

How may a horse be prepared for a constant supply of salt, and what are the advantages of it?

How often should a horse be groomed?
What is a good instrument for this purpose?

Is a sharp currycomb severe and should its use about the head be avoided?

What is the best help for grooming in shedding time?
How may matted, frozen fetlocks be cleaned?
Should they be cut?
Why should a horse be cleaned outside the stable?
What injuries result from damp floors?
Is it important to have a well lighted stable?
Does a horse need pure air?

Is the reflection of light from snow hard on a horse's eyes?

Does a horse need a level surface to stand upon?

How may drainage and comfort to the horse both be secured?

What is the safest and most comfortable way to fasten a horse in his stall?

If he must be tied, what should be the length of his halter?

How may horses be safely taken from a burning building?

What about the fit of a harness?

What points need attention?

What effect do frosty bits have on a horse's mouth?

How may they be warmed?

What injuries result from the use of the tight check-rein?

What are some of the evils of blinders?

Is not the freedom from shying horses in Russia strong evidence that blinders should not be used?

Who denounce check-reins and blinders?

What bits should be avoided?

How should a long drive be managed?

How drive up and down hill?

Are poverty and overwork excuses for cruelty?

Look up the story of Midas and the golden touch.

What is the golden touch that all may have?

CHAPTER XXXV.
THE MULE AND THE BURRO.
"Ich dien," I serve.

This motto immortalized Prince John. In lifting up this great sentiment he sought to show the royalty of service; his great soul laid claim to nobility, not because of birth, not because of lands and titles, but because of service, and the world has long adjudged his claim the *best*. How, then, can we deny honor to the patient, serving mule, and the little burro, the faithful of the faithful? These creatures are unwearying in their toil for us, and with an ingratitude hard to understand, we overwhelm them with contempt and ridicule. The pig is the only other domestic animal that we have so wantonly bemeaned, but he does not work for us as does the mule. Much of our treatment of these helpers, looks like giving blows for blessings. Yet those who have taken the trouble to observe tell us mules are more sagacious than horses. They were not always held in such contempt. The time was when they drew royal cars. Sure footed, steady nerved, they have ever been worthy of great trusts. The time of the domestication of the ass, like that of the horse, is lost in the dimness of history; and, like the horse, possibly those found wild to-day, are descendants of individuals escaped from civilization. In mountainous and barren districts of Central and Southern India these spirited creatures subsist where as many rabbits would almost starve. Fleet and beautiful, Job's description of them still holds good. [Job, xxxix: 5-8.]

As in the case of the hog, man's contact with the ass has wrought him ill. Hard work, hard fare, hard words, and too often hard blows have been his lot. Under such treatment naturally enough he has become less spirited and less graceful and beautiful in proportion. We have an instructive exception to this in Spain, where the ass and the hybrid mule are treated with much more respect and care than in most other countries; and there it has its highest development. The mild climate, no doubt, has something to do with it. It is clear that they do not thrive so well in cold northern climates. But kind, intelligent treatment certainly is an important factor in this improved condition. So the interests of a better humanity, as well as better beasts of burden, demand a change in the treatment of this class of animals.

The remarkable intelligence of the mule should give him favor with man. The mule Denver, the humorist of Prof. Bristol's school of horses, certainly understood himself when he rang the bell furiously to stop his master's drinking in imitation of the check the master put upon him. His affectionate attention to the pretty little white pony, Lotty, when she fell into disgrace for inattention during the drill, is something to teach tender consideration to higher minds.

Prince John had his motto, "Ich Dien," emblazoned upon a banner which he carried with him unto death. The mule lifts up the same great principle in *perpetuo* with his race. Mule means to moil or toil, and gallantly as Prince John, many of them have fallen in service. But they have not won honor as did he.

Every schoolboy that has a sense of chivalry should speak and work for better treatment of these downtrodden creatures. Longfellow says:

"Among the noblest in the land,
Though he may count himself the least,
That man I honor and revere
Who, without favor, without fear,
In the wide country dares to stand
The *friend* of *every friendless beast.*"

The burro is a conspicuous figure in the life of the Rocky Mountains. For freighting over rough and rugged ways this sturdy, sagacious little helper is unequalled. Agile, sure footed, strong, enduring; climbing like a goat and faithful as a dog; without a bridle and without a driver he carries burdens to places inaccessible to the horse. The

mines of that region must have been much slower and
more expensive of development without the burro. He
picks his way over rocky and precipitous trails with the
care and discrimination of a man. There are many instances of their wisdom and humor. This tribe is more
given to choosing a leader than are horses. One owner
insisted that his lead burro knew the days of the week.
On Sunday he would graze sociably with the herd, but on
Monday morning he was only to be found in some secret
cañon, or mountain pocket in solitary seclusion.

The quick wit and quick sympathy of the mule makes
him keenly sensible of injustice and contempt, and this it
is, no doubt, that gives him the air of stolid indifference
and obstinacy, so frequently remarked. The most sensitive metal is the most easily warped. As we grow in appreciation of true service, and rank it as the noblest end
of life, we must grow in appreciation of these faithful
helpers who give so much and ask so little. Hardier than
the horse, stronger for their weight, they require less food
and less care.

"TO A YOUNG ASS."—S. T. COLERIDGE.

Its mother being tethered near it.

" Poor little foal of an oppressed race!
I love the languid patience of thy face;
And oft with gentle hand I give thee bread,
And clap thy ragged coat and pat thy head.
But what thy dulled spirits hath dismayed,
That never thou dost sport along the glade;
And most unlike the nature of things young,

That earthward still thy nerveless head is hung?
Do thy prophetic fears anticipate,
Meek child of misery! thy future fate,
Thy starving meal, and all the thousand aches
That patient merit of the unworthy takes?

" Or is thy sad heart thrilled with filial pain
To see thy wretched mother's shortened chain?
And truly, very piteous is her lot,
Chained to a log within a narrow spot
Where the close-eaten grass is scarcely seen,
While sweet around her waves the tempting green.

" Poor ass! thy master should have learned to show
Pity, best taught by fellowship of woe:
For much I fear me that he lives like thee
Half-famished in a land of luxury.
How askingly its footsteps hither bend!
It seems to say: And have I, then, one friend?
Innocent foal! thou poor, despised, forlorn!
I hail thee, brother, spite of the fool's scorn,
And fain would take thee with me, in the dell
Of peace and mild equality to dwell.

" Where toil shall call the charmer health his bride,
And laughter tickle plenty's ribless side.
How thou wouldst toss thy heels in gamesome play,
And frisk about as lamb or kitten gay!
Yea? and more musically sweet to me
Thy dissonant harsh bray of joy would be
Than warbled melodies that soothe to rest
The aching of pale fashion's vacant breast."

QUESTIONS.

What is the motto of this lesson?
Look up Prince John and his motto.
Look up the early history of the ass and mule.
In what countries have they been most appreciated and reached their highest development?
What is the general feeling toward the mule in this country?
What does mule mean?
Was Prince John distinguished because he was born a prince, or because he held up a great principle?
If he won honor in service, does not the mule earn our respect, at least, by his patient toil?
Commit Longfellow's lines.
Does this call for defense for the overburdened, abused mule?
Are burros especially useful in the Rocky Mountains?
What are some of their points of advantage over the horse?
Does the intelligence and sensitiveness of the mule make him resent injustice?
Study carefully the poem "To a Young Ass."
How many pleasant traits does the poet attribute to this foal?
How many lessons does he give us in kindness?

CHAPTER XXXVI.
THE COMMON HEN.

"Kindness is the Music of the World."

" The careful hen
Calls all her chirping family around,
Fed and defended by the fearless cock
Whose breast with ardor flames."
James Thompson.

The most thoroughly domesticated of all the feathered tribe is our common hen. It comes to us from Central Asia, the native land of nearly all the animals man has tamed.

Thousands of years ago, in the groves of the far off plains of Iran, there were companies of birds that lived together in loving way, after the manner of patriarchal families. They were very skillful at scratching up worms and seeds from the leaf mold; could even tear up the earth for succulent roots. They gave over flying for the most part, except a sort of winged run or a flutter into trees for hiding from near and sudden danger. Their plumage was very beautiful in the sunshine, giving out the dazzling, shimmering lights of jewels.

The brave and gallant cock gave the world examples of chivalry. The choicest product of all his scratching was set forth with a joyful note of invitation to his flock, and with gallant abstinence he watched them eat it up. He would do battle valiantly with bird or beast threatening the safety of him or his. His long spurs were effective weapons, and he used them with wonderful skill and courage. Most of his neighbors of the field and wood, even though many times his size, dreaded an encounter with him.

One day a half wild boy, who loved to wander in the woods and make friends with the creatures there, found a brooding mother bird that held her six small eggs so dear, fear could not drive her from them. The boy admired her courage, and with a friendly chirp, flung her a handful of seeds he had stripped from the grass along his way. She received this courtesy rather doubtfully, and yet received, for she was hungry, yet must shield her treasures.

Again and again he came bringing her seeds and berries; by and by her natural sympathy overcame her fears, and she picked trustingly out of the friendly hand. One day she let him stroke her, and the next he had her, nest and all, in his cap, and carried her to his simple home.

The poor hen, though troubled, was loyal to her nest, for she had heard a pecking beneath her breast and knew her chicks would soon nestle warm against her heart. So they did, almost before she ceased to tremble, and she lost much of her fear in joy and care for these downy things.

Her captor and his little sister delighted in them, too. They fed the pretty brood so well, and were so gentle with them always that by and by their shyness wore away. The children fenced them in and clipped their wings, and afterwards they found other eggs and other chicks, which added to the flock.

The children's mother found it good to have a sure supply of eggs at hand, and encouraged this bird raising. So it was that the work of helping each other on toward civilization began between the hen and man; began, perhaps, in many different families in much the same way, for boys and girls were always fond of pets, and these fowls were easily won because of their quick sympathy.

Century after century the work has gone on with much giving and taking on both sides. Men have grown better because they cared for something outside of themselves, and gained large bounty for the table.

The birds grew from six to ten-fold larger, more productive and more expressive. In their native state they had few notes with which to speak their mind, but those who have made close friends with them say that our hens to-day have as many as twenty distinct calls expressing different feelings and desires. This is to human ears; we don't know how many variations are understood among themselves.

It is an easy and pleasant thing for boys and girls to keep a chicken park. Hens, rightly cared for, lay eggs enough to pay for all their feed, furnish some to eat and spending money besides. Wyandottes are tame as petted pigeons; even the shy brownie shows affection for its mistress, and the great Brahma, that stands up almost as tall as a turkey, likes to be stroked as it picks its grain.

The fierce fighting spirit has left the cock with advancing civilization, but he still keeps a gallant guardianship over his flock. If need arise he will defend them bravely. He still calls the hens to take the choice fruits of his scratching, unless he has grown old and selfish.

These birds are so attached to human society that they no longer have a wish to wander off and live apart. Even in warm countries, where the wilderness would yield them abundant food, they have never run wild. They are very remarkable in this. Other domestic animals, except the dog, go wild under favorable circumstances; some with half a chance. The hen may steal her nest away, but she keeps close to some dwelling. She will go with man into any land, endure summer or winter, wind or rain, and bless him with her bounty. The egg is the neatest package of food Nature has put up for man. It is remarkable that the egg of every known bird is wholesome and nourishes the body quickly.

These fowls, that give us so much affectionate good will along with their material benefits, claim our kindly care.

Prof. N. S. Shaler, of Harvard University, says that town boys and girls would be better for having animals to care for, and recommends chickens as the most valuable and useful. He thinks that responsibility for their well being and comfort, study of their varied notes and habits, will make the sympathies and kindly impulses of our boys and girls grow so much, that selfishness and oppression of fellow beings may die out of the hearts of our growing men and women.

The Harvard professor is right. Good care of these birds will make us better. Right care means that hen houses must be kept clean, so the chickens may be healthy. Fresh water must be kept within easy reach, and the water vessels and feeding troughs must be thoroughly cleaned every day, or diseases will spring up among the flock.

In warm weather it is surprising how much hens will drink. Like people, they will drink more and oftener. They may be kept in close quarters if great attention is given to cleanliness. Dust for the dust bath and room for lively scratching are important. See that they have warm winter quarters and plenty of light, with a chance to roost near the roof.

Like sheep, hens know their master's voice and gaily run at his call. The good master and mistress come to know and respond to the hen's notes of content, ecstacy, alarm, distress, affection, and satisfaction.

This story of a Black Spanish chick indicates quick understanding, if not reason, and a social nature not to be denied:

THE STORY OF BLACKY.

He was an orphan, black and downy, given to a White Leghorn hen, who had a brood of white fluffs with shiny, yellow bills. It ill-chanced that she was a selfish mother and would not adopt poor Blacky. She was, indeed, bitter against him, and pecked at him angrily, refusing him so much as a morsel of food at her table or a moment's shelter beneath her ample wings.

Though a wee bird, Blacky was plucky and cheery. He took to his mates and his mates took to him, thinking, no doubt, that his black set off their white to a charm.

Under the insistent protection of his mistress Blacky got through the first few days with only a few bruises and a lame foot, from the sharp bill of this unwilling mother. He dreaded her displeasure, but nothing could induce him to give up his place with the brood, and he soon went ahead of his mistress in looking out for himself. Much forced exercise made his legs strong and swift, and whenever he saw the hen glance toward him he made a run that would do honor to his remote kindred, the ostrich, so famed for speed.

His tactful mistress learned to favor him by putting the food down close to a tree that shaded the chicken park. He would conceal himself behind the tree until mother Biddy was fully occupied with satisfying her own hunger, then slip up and silently make haste to get his share. Appetite, however, never so distracted his attention but he could forecast an intended movement, and, like a flash, make for safety. If the sun hid its face or the wind blew cold, and Biddy called her family to the shelter of her hovering wings, Blacky dared not run with the rest. He shivered afar off, uttering piteous, homesick cries that would have melted a heart of stone, but Biddy had hardened hers seven times and she was unmoved. When she had the little white balls all cuddled close to her breast and had drawn her head down for a full-content nap, he hushed every sound, and slipping softly up behind, crouched low and ran under her. So she gave a blessing and knew it not, and he was thankful and grew apace.

Nor would she allow him to go into the coop with the rest, but when all was quiet he would steal to the door and edge slowly in. If Biddy chanced to be facing him and awake, there was an angry cry and an ugly thrust of her beak, and poor Blacky would fly, shrieking with fright. Then he would hang about again, sad and lonely, till the friendly shadows deepened enough for him to creep unnoticed into the coop under the unwilling wings.

By and by, when Biddy left them all to lay another nest full of eggs, as was her wont, Blacky and his mates had happy, peaceful times together in the coop and under the tree. "Nothing succeeds like success."

Watching Blacky gave his mistress new ideas of the intelligence of fowls, and it made her more careful to understand and satisfy the needs of all her flock. When asked what she would urge as most important for their kindly care, she said quickly: "Don't let them lack for fresh water." Remember that "thoughtlessness is selfish, and selfishness is sin."

QUESTIONS.

What is the motto?
How long since the taming of our common barn-yard fowls began?
What kind of a bird did they come from?
Have they been changed by domestication?
Has domestication made them larger?
Has it made them lay more?
Has it made them more sensitive?
What has man gained from his care of them?
Is chicken raising profitable at the present time?

May children take care of fowls?

What does Prof. N. S. Shaler say about the moral benefits that children may gain from right care of animals?

What does he especially recommend for town children?

What are some of the important details of kindly care?

How many different calls have these fowls that the attentive human ear has detected?

Let the boys and girls make a study of this and see how many they can distinguish in a few weeks.

What important change has cultivation brought to the character of the cock?

Tell the story of Blacky.

How did he manifest intelligence and sensibility?

What did his mistress learn from him?

Give the closing quotation of this chapter.

CHAPTER XXXVII.
DOMESTIC WATER FOWLS.
Geese, Ducks, and Swans.

"Those who rest on eider down,
 Taking borrowed ease,
 Owe a tribute of sweet care
 To the wild wings of the seas."

"Whither midst falling dew, while glow the heavens
  With the last steps of day,
 Far through their rosy depths dost thou pursue
  Thy solitary way.

"Vainly the fowler's eye
  Might mark thy distant flight to do thee wrong,
 As darkly painted on the crimson sky,
  Thy figure floats along.

"He, who from zone to zone,
  Guides thine unerring flight,
 Through the long way that I must tread alone,
  Will guide my steps aright."—*Bryant.*

Make a study of the flights of ducks and geese that go over your head spring and autumn, and you will have new ideas of their intelligence, their beauty and their skill. With geese it is always a game of "follow your leader." The leader (whether chosen by reason of strength or grace, or wisdom, we know not) heads the company in kingly style. Sometimes they arrange themselves in a single, long line, but oftener they form a letter V with the point in front. See how they move; perfect ranks, even distances, never any crowding, never any clashing of wings, though their course should be suddenly turned aside, checked, or borne backward. What swift understanding! What perfect poise! What astonishing skill! A panic is impossible whatever surprise or danger they may meet. Have they a fine rhythmic sense that catches the meaning of changes in the pulsating air like an electric flash? Those who have tried keeping step in companies of forty or fifty in a schoolroom know that intelligent care and close attention on the part of every one is necessary for straight lines and exact changes, even after much special drill. How often the distances are lost and the lines broken. Then how shall we measure the mind that achieves the perfect march in spite of greater difficulties? This ought to give flattering meaning to the phrase, "like a goose."

Ducks and geese are easily domesticated, and were among the early possessions of men. But the spirit of migration that is strong upon them makes against the complete attachment to the homestead that we see in the hen. Perhaps this is one reason they have changed so little, and so readily return to their wild state. About lakes and ponds they thrive and are very happy.

Ducks are poor walkers; their legs are set so far back on their bodies; but on the water, darting, floating, diving, the play of light bringing out a whole symphony of color from their iridescent plumage, they teach grace and harmony of bodily expression. The young of all our domestic fowls are beautiful, and the Pekin duckling heads the list. It is a symphony in yellow; the deeper, stronger tone of the bill and delicately webbed foot imperceptibly blending into the lighter translucent amber of the body. Sunlit topaz may be like it in some small measure. But topaz has no power to cuddle and caress, to bill and pipe sweet love notes. Two little children first made me acquainted with these fair creatures, and life has been brighter ever since. Under the training of these children the baby ducks learned many things quite remarkable, the most helpful of which was catching flies. Held in reach by their little master and mistress they cleared the windows day after day. This was in their line, as ducks are largely animal feeders. Another thing of curious interest these children showed me; their ducks, big and little, went to bed upon the still surface of the pool. They were in a locality infested with troublesome vermin, rats and weasels, and these birds made themselves safe from such enemies by anchoring well out from land when the twilight fell, tucking their heads under their wings and sleeping the sleep of the care-free. Whether their anchor was gravity, magnetism, or something yet unnamed, we never knew. One night a high wind blew them close to shore, as the children discovered in the early morning.

All this happened in a mild climate, but one unusually cold morning the feathered fleet awoke to find arrows and lances of ice over the surface of the water. Their little friends called to them anxiously, guessing from the ache in their own fingers and toes that the pretty orange feet of their pets must be frozen. But the ducks came to their proffered breakfast with as unsatisfiable appetites as ever, chattering together in a sort of ecstacy, as if this unexpected north wind had brought them new joy. Their waterproof coats and their high temperature kept them warm.

Wordsworth's description of the wild duck's nest discloses some of the beauty with which the world is filled: "Heaven lies about us in our infancy," hidden only from those who seeing, do not see; and hearing, do not hear, because they are cold hearted and selfish.

"THE WILD DUCK'S NEST.

" The imperial consort of the fairy king
   Owns not a sylvan bower or gorgeous cell,
   With emerald floored, and with purpureal shell
   Ceilinged and roofed that is so fair a thing
   As this low structure.

" Words cannot paint the o'ershadowing yew tree bough
   And dimly-gleaming nest—a hollow crown
   Of golden leaves inlaid with silver down,
   Fine as the mother's softest plumes allow;
   I gazed—and, self-accused while gazing, sighed
   For human kind, weak slave of cumbrous pride."

Geese do not have the lustrous, changeable colors of the duck, but their legs are placed further forward, enabling them to walk with ease. This gives them advantages in grazing over fields. They are chiefly vegetarians and will crop nearly as much grass in a day as a half grown sheep.

A great many remarkable anecdotes are told about the goose, which, whether true or not, go to prove that this bird has won a large place for herself in the interest of those with whom she has been associated. The flock of geese that aroused the sleepy sentinel when an enemy was scaling the Capitoline hill, bound the Romans to them, and to their kind, in grateful reverence.

These water fowls cannot be kept in close quarters, as hens. They must have plenty of water and pasturage. But with these, and intelligent, kindly care, they give back generously to man. Domesticated, they thrive best in the temperate zone. Their young mature in a few months and Chambers' Encyclopedia tells of a gander that lived to the good old age of eighty years. Their soft feathers are in great demand for beds and cushions. Whoever takes this close, warm coat for his own creature comforts, should be mindful of the season, give good shelter from untimely storms, and see that pain is not inflicted by the picking.

A modern poet, who has caught the music and the meaning of the gosling's happy chatter, has given it to us in a poem, "My Sleepy Goslings." I give it here to help us understand them and to incline us kindly to them:

"MY SLEEPY GOSLINGS."—FLORA E. BENNETT.

Oh, say, did you ever listen,
   Oh, say, did you ever try
To understand what the goslings say,
In their vesper hymns, at close of day,
Their "baby sleep," their roundelay,
   Their "good night" lullaby?

After a long day's journey,
   The whole of the weary brood
Come trudging home, with pattering feet,
Telling, in accents grave and sweet,
Of wonderful victories and defeat,
   While they were seeking food.

They all drop down in a circle,
    And chatter of strangest things,
Of the bumblebee, with his velvet crest,
And the rumbly-buzz within his vest—
They tell how the fire-fly builds her nest,
    And the moth, with silken wings—

And how, in the early morning,
    While seeking the clover's bloom,
They wrestled with dandelion tops,
And chased a funny bird that hops,
Then drank the silvery dew that drops
    Down from the spider's loom.

They tell of strange adventures
    With bugs as black as night,
And how a great green ugly frog
Made faces at them from a log,
And then jumped back into the bog—
    Which gave them such a fright!

But now, that the day is over—
    And they are free from harm—
They chirp with drowsy, dense delight,
With closing eyes to the falling night,
Huddling together close and tight—
    Together snug and warm.

And then they begin to murmur
    A musical "all is well"—
A fairy hears it and echoes the strain,
Another one catches and sends it again
To a third, who gathers the whole refrain
    In the folds of his silver bell.

Peep low, my pretty goslings,
  Soft trills the nightingale;
The dew is falling, the crickets sing,
The fire-fly dances, the swamp mists cling,
A fairy poises on gossamer wing—
  "All's right, and all is well."

Sweeter than lamentation
  Of autumn's turtle-dove!
Sweeter than dirge to the falling leaves,
  So solemnly sung by October's breeze,
Or cadence of the sorrowful trees,
  Mourning for desolate love!

Sweeter than rippling waters,
  Or the notes of the dying swan!
Sweeter than robin, or whip-poor-will,
  Is that "rock-a-bye" from fairy hill,
That sweet refrain of "Peace be still,"
  Which the goslings coo and murmur and trill,
From evening until dawn.

THE SWAN.

Swans we meet with only upon the lakelet in our parks. Their long, arched necks, their uplifted wings, the shimmer of their plumage, their perfect grace of movement upon the water make them a thing of joy and beauty. They are friendly and will take a bunch of clover or a cookey from a gentle hand. Kindness is the golden passport, the sesame that opens the way to familiar and sympathetic relations with them as with all other animals. Early voyagers to Australia tell us that at first the geese there stood thick upon the shore to welcome them, naturally being drawn toward man. When such confidence was cruelly destroyed we can't wonder that kindness and good will must be long proven to win back a little trust.

The soft notes of the swan are very sweet when she is talking to her cygnets. When she takes them a ride on her back her chant, despite her little variety of tone, rises to a beauty worthy of the praise accorded it from olden times.

QUESTIONS.

What is the motto of this lesson?
What three domestic birds have we from the same family of water fowls?
See the encyclopedia for the distinctions of the three.
Are any of these greatly changed by domestication?
What tendency makes against domesticating them so completely as the hen?
What can you say of their intelligence?
Describe a flight of geese.
How does its order compare with the march of school boys and girls?
Commit Bryan's lines "To a Water Fowl."
Why do ducks and geese walk so differently?
Would it be cruel to try to make a duck run?
Is the Pekin duckling especially beautiful?
Tell about the children's ducks.
What are the special needs of these water fowls?
Are the feathers of ducks and geese in great demand?
What points should be observed in picking them?
What are the great attractions of the swan?
Does kindness readily win the confidence of all these birds?

CHAPTER XXXVIII.

TURKEYS, GUINEAS AND PEA FOWLS.

"Lie low at the feet of beauty, *that*, ever shall abide."
Jean Ingelow.

The turkey enjoys the distinction of being the only domestic animal that the new world has given to civilization, and it was sent to the old world to be tamed. The North American Indian, like other savages, no doubt, often made pets of the wild creatures of the forest; hatching their young and rearing them for the pleasure and advantage of their companionship. With the llama and alpaca something like domestic relations seem to have been established so that they became to a degree burden-bearers, but as soon as they could escape from the controlling hand, they returned to their mountain fastnesses, and to-day they show no trace of this passing submission. However, though the Indian counted the wild turkey choice game, he apparently never thought of taming it. Soon after the thrill of change, felt by this continent when the Santa Maria touched its shore, some of the voyagers took turkeys back to Spain, as specimens of the large and beautiful birds of the wonderful new world, and there they were domesticated, being made much of in parts of Europe and England for many years. Like the indifferent husband who fell deeply in love with his wife on spending an evening with her in a brilliant company away from home, the American was taken with the turkey in Europe, and brought it back home again to be a standby of the barnyard when he might have caught it from the forest hard by his door, and tamed it easily.

Though easily won to domestication it seems but little more than half won yet. Its wild companions can readily entice it into the woods again, but it is one of the gentlest and most sympathetic of all our barnyard tribes. Refined, applied to it, is not a misplaced adjective. Little turkeys, when taken in the hand, have a cuddling movement and a soft content note, very endearing. No one has ever discovered exactly why the dew is so blighting to the baby turkey, but it is an empirical law that a few pearly drops of morning dew brushed from grass or shrub is quite enough to lay it low, as if they were drops of venom. So great care must be taken to keep them dry. The mother turkey talks very sweetly to her brood and tends them with anxious care, but when sitting she never pecks the hand thrust beneath her breast to take out a warm, freckled egg, or a fresh hatched bird, as does frequently the more domestic hen. A shy respect seems to tinge her manner towards man. It would be called dove-like if she were not so large a bird. Man has never yet learned the conditions under which young turkeys thrive. Chickens, ducks, and geese are easily reared, but turkeys are very tender before they are fledged, though apparently hardy afterwards. No doubt a close and friendly study of their habits in their native woods would discover some important conditions for their welfare that are lacking in domestic surroundings. Such a study might mature the sympathetic relation between men and turkeys; at present it falls far short of fullness, though in many ways the turkey seems to invite greater nearness. They like free range in wooded pastures, and the young do best in such liberty. Trees are their favorite roosting places. It goes almost as hard with them to be forced to take shelter in a house as it did with Leatherstocking. The gobbler, especially of the large bronze breed, is one of the most splendidly beautiful of large birds, ranking only second to the peacock. With his tail spread, strutting in the sun, he is a laughable picture of vanity, but is, at the same time, an ornament to any grounds. Vanity is always selfish, and so it happens that he is not so gallant to his flock as is our "chanticleer." Turkeys, even in domestication, move about in a flock. Hens are very social creatures, but, like people, they don't mind going their several separate ways in pursuit of a livelihood, day after day.

The guinea is one of Africa's few contributions to our domestic life. This pretty, lead-colored, polka-dotted creature is even more shy than the turkey. The young hide like little quails and are as graceful and beautiful in form and movement. They are great layers and their small, quail-shaped, bronze-brown eggs are very fine in quality. "Put-rack" is the clear, incessant call of these birds, and it is better than a scare-crow to keep hawks out of the chicken park; but a whole flock of them make an almost deafening noise. They still bear traces of barbarism in a quarelsome disposition. They are likely to make life a burden to associated poultry. But thorough civilization will doubtless eradicate this and soften their voices. This is a development worth trying for. They are in so many ways an attractive bird, with taking, piquant manners. As yet the tendency to steal their nests, hatch their young apart, and run half wild, greatly lessens their economic value.

But systematic, persevering, intelligent kindness is a marvelous taming power. It is worth while to try it on this pretty bird.

The peacock comes to us from India, where it luxuriates, especially in southern parts. The peahen is modestly attired, but the cock, with his tail spread, its dazzling eyes making a splendid rainbow|in the sun—irridescent, changeful hues, glancing like arrows from every plume—is one of the most magnificent and gorgeous sights in nature. Thousands of years ago the ancients held this royal bird in high favor, and took him captive, but his domestication does not yet approach perfection. He is a vain bird, not only glorying in his tail, but evidently delighting also in his rasping, monotonous voice. His tail, we should remember, is not a true tail at all, but an exagerated development of the tail covers, which, when erected are supported by the true tail from behind. The beautiful eye of these feathers has been a most effective motive in art. Whistler, the artist, decorated the dining-room in one of the wealthy homes in London with the peacock eye running as a motive throughout the whole—walls, curtains, upholstering and table furnishing. It is accounted one of the most beautiful art works of our time. The peacock is profitable to us for beauty alone. He does not give us close friendship, whether because of selfishness on his part (vanity is selfishness) or because of man's selfish approach of him, we cannot tell.

He likes to be near our homes, being well content in a woody park close by, where he can take an occasional promenade with spreading tail across a house lawn, but he does not favor familiarity.

It is said that people who live together, come to look alike. By the time the golden wedding rolls around husband and wife are likely to bear a marked resemblance. There is no doubt but animals are impressed with the mental and moral qualities of their masters. Like begets like. Gentle manners, gentle tones, honest care, and just requirements, a sympathetic approach, and an unvarying kindness may accomplish unforeshadowed things, in winning all helpful and beautiful creatures into complete alliance with us for the world's work. So study them and work with them from the standpoint of friends; the birds are most responsive because most sympathetic, and it is the easiest field of study and work for boys and girls. Wherever you are, however limited your resources, you can have some share in this pleasure and blessing. If you are in a crowded city where you absolutely have no spot of ground and want a pet, don't get a bird and prison it; there must be sparrows or pigeons lodged some place near; if you can't put out a box for them at your roof window, you can make friends with them along the street. Some crumbs of bread, any waste from the table, they will receive gratefully. Learn where they live and how they live. Study their invidualily, always with respectful approach, such as you would accord a human being whose acquaintance you coveted as a pleasure and an honor. "One man may lead a horse to water, but twenty men can't make him drink." This is a pithy proverb. Friendship can't be forced, but kindness and good will never fail to win it, where it is worth the winning. Try to establish in some measure a responsible care of some creature, that you may give and get a blessing.

Wherever it is possible, put up bird houses for the martins and bluebirds, as well as pigeons. A box sixteen by eighteen inches, with a door at one corner, so the nest may be hid from view, will make good house room for a pair of pigeons, and still smaller quarters will accommodate the others. Invite them by your tactful interest, and in grounds where you have jurisdiction never allow them to be thrown at or teased or spoken rudely to, much less shot at. A lady was once favored by the nesting of a wren in her back porch. It had such confidence in her before the summer was over, that it would sit upon the nest and look at her in friendliest fashion when she stood right beside it. She might have stroked its glossy coat, no doubt, but she was too respectful to take liberties. Her movements about it were always gentle, and she was careful that it never heard harsh tones or had a fright in that back porch. Boys and girls may make for themselves such refining friendships if they will be as companionable.

If you can get a patch of ground six feet square, keep a half dozen hens upon it. Get books and papers and learn just how to do it. They will make you rich in more ways than one. Be sure you keep their quarters scrupulously neat, and make as determined a fight against vermin among them as for yourself. Anything short of this is cruelty as well as loss. If you are in a rural town or country place, stretch out the boundaries of your park and increase their numbers accordingly. If you have lake or spring or water course at your command, with pasturage, add geese and ducks to your possessions. Hens like grass and green things, too. If you have wooded land, get turkeys, and see if you can help to solve the problem of their more complete domestication. If you have missionary zeal, get guineas, and try to civilize their tempers and their voices. If you are rich, add the peacock to your list. Study them each and all for their good and yours. Learn to observe accurately, remembering all the while that nature's children yield their secrets and their confidence only to the loving and the patient, and you will lay foundations of natural history study that will be priceless.

QUESTIONS.

What is the motto of this lesson?
What is the only domestic animal native to America?
What of the disposition of the turkey?
As we have it in domestication, how do the old and young differ in hardiness?
What special care do they need?
What of the beauty of the gobbler?
What of his character?
What kind of roost do they prefer?
What country gave us the guinea fowl?
What is its character?
What of its eggs?
Describe the young.
What of the guinea temper and voice?
Is there any reason to hope that thorough domestication might subdue both of these, and is it worth while to try for it?
Look up the change wrought on animals by domestication.
Of what country is the peacock native?

See who can give the fullest description of the peacock eye and its use in art.

Is the peacock of early domestication?

Is it on terms of intimacy with man?

What is its present value to us?

Let each make a careful study of what constitutes right care of the fowl that interests him or her most.

May every one, rich or poor, find some opportunity to get and give in this way.

What may one do, who has no patch of ground or sky for a bird house or hen coop?

Look up in poultry journals and hand books what may be done with hens on six feet square.

CHAPTER XXXIX.
PIGEONS, PARROTS, AND SONG BIRDS.
"The Group Built for Joy."

"When in a May-day hush
Chanteth the Missel thrush
The harp o'the heart makes answer with murmurous stirs."—*Jean Ingelow.*

"The group built for joy" is a happy description of birds. With a temperature two degrees higher than that of man, with bodies cunningly devised for sailing "the illimitable air," with a love for the beautiful that makes him an artist in sound, and form, and color, "the bird is a mystic poet, half celestial, half earthly, flying over ocean and mountain heights, across continents, in all latitudes." "Built for joy" indeed! Hear the ecstasy in the mocking bird's trill, the meadow lark's warble, the swallow's twitter, the pewee's soft notes, the martin's chatter and the quail's clear call. Even the caged canary has a rapture in his song which Mrs. Muloch Craik says tells men the secret of a happy life.

"Howsoe'er thy lot's assigned,
Meet it with a cheerful mind."

Their emotional nature is very large, and they evidently see the world on its heavenward side. It fills them with a delight which their flexible voices, their harmony of motion, their sweep of earth and sky, are not enough to express. All these combined, leave them with volumes of unuttered feeling on a sweet spring morning.

Birds marry truly. Some of them, as pigeons and paroquets, pair off, taking their companions for better or for worse while life shall last. Indeed, some who must know, tell us that certain loving bird hearts break at the loss of a mate, so that death to one means death to both. It is popularly believed that the turtle-dove, when uttering her tender, plaintive, cooing note, is mourning for her lost mate, but this is only her word of solemn, sweet content in the blessed summer time.

The great pigeon tribe are singularly faithful, mate to mate, and their billing and cooing has become a type of demonstrative affection the world around. Domestication does not change this homey, pairing habit, as in the case of ducks and geese. Mr. and Mrs. Dove will set up housekeeping in a dovecote, and while sharing freely in the social pleasures of the neighborhood, will care for each other, and their family, in their third story flat, it may be, with full measure of content. They go down to happy old age side by side. But their instincts are so fine that unless the dovecote is kept clean and made pleasing to the eye by an occasional coat of paint (white is preferred) they will seek other quarters. So in town or country if we would have these charming friends about us, we must help them realize their ideals of neatness. Their grace of form, the iridescent lights that play about the head and neck, their shy trust, their gentle bearing, make them an ornament to any street or grounds, and a heart culture to the people with whom they are associated.

If you live in town you can have the full pleasure of

them as in the country you have the pleasure of the lark
and thrush, at the simple cost of opening ears and eyes
and heart. A little expenditure of kindness upon them
yields large returns. A handful of grain, some scraps
from the table, wins their confidence and affection, which
is, no doubt, on the same principle that a good dinner
puts a man at peace with all the world.

The dove has long been established as the emblem
of purity, of peace, of love, and spiritual power. As a
sign of peace she always bears an olive branch in her
mouth.

"THE DOVES OF VENICE."—LAURA WINTHROP JOHNSON.

 I stood in the quiet piazza,
  Where come rude noises never;
 But the feet of children, the wings of doves,
  Are sounding on forever.

 And the cooing of their soft voices,
  And the touch of the rippling sea,
 And the ringing clock of the armed knight,
  Came through the noon to me.

 While their necks with rainbow gleaming,
  'Neath the dark old arches shone,
 And the campanile's shadow long,
  Moved o'er the pavement stone.

 And from every "coigne of vantage,"
  Where lay some hidden nest,
 They fluttered, peeped, and glistened forth,
  Sacred, serene, at rest.

I thought of thy saint, O Venice!
  Who said in his tenderness,
"I love thy birds, my Father dear,
  Our lives they cheer and bless!

"For love is not for men only;
  To the tiniest little things
Give room to nestle in our hearts;
  Give freedom to all wings!"

And the lovely, still piazza,
  Seemed with his presence blest,
And I, and the children, and the dove,
  Partakers of His rest.

Every one must look upon the pigeon more affectionately and care for it more tenderly, after reading this poem. They are so common and so easily won to intimacy, it is a pity any boy or girl should miss the character growth and refinement that kindly, intelligent care of them brings.

Parrots make up in splendid color and mind power what they lack in musical art. Their voices are, for the most part, harsh and discordant. But we forgive them that, when they greet us in our own language and recognize a bit of humor with a distinctively human laugh. It is not their imitative skill alone that indicates a high order of intelligence. As household pets they unmistakably show a large understanding of the family life, its hopes, its joys and its sorrows, and they have been trained to remarkable mechanical skill.

Their magnificent plumage, changeable green, blue and red, make them a coveted decoration in many homes.

Some individuals are much quicker and brighter than others. They are docile and affectionate. They often manifest the willfulness, iritability and obstinacy that are observable sometimes in boys and girls (the more the pity), but if care is taken to prevent their being worried, teased or cheated, to keep them smooth tempered, they may go down to a green old age a joy and comfort to their friends. It is said that some parrots have lived a hundred years, so it is, they see much of life.

From freedom and home joys we take larks, linnets, canaries, and mocking birds, shut them up in cages, that they may sing for us and set off our rooms with their beauty, and then sometimes forget their necessities, not to say their comforts. We forget their needed bath, forget their sand, forget they need variety, forget their seed even, forget the open cage and the untaught cat, forget the needed protection on a cold night, forget the bird is a social little creature, loving companionship of its own kind, forget its rapture in the sunlight, forget its delight in flowers and trees, and then think to set all right with the self-excusing phrase, " I forgot," or " I didn't know."

" And God, who notes the sparrow's fall, wilt *Thou* the sinless sufferer's pain forget?"—*Holmes.*

Sometimes the poor little birds are killed by our forgetting and not knowing; but even if they live on, how many of their joys we have killed.

What a beautiful meaning it would give to our relations with the birds, as well as other animals, if our superior intelligence and skill co-operated with nature to work out the full harmony of joy, that with infinite variation runs as a definite motive throughout the universe. Love and kindness may lend to very little children's hands an Orpheus-touch that can thrill the heart strings of all life with divinest music, blending in perfect harmony all notes of joy.

Selfishness and ignorance are cruel, and cruelty is jangling discord. Let us study to be wise in loving service; forgetting, no, *not one*, save self.

"Then every tender, living thing,
Shall feed by streams of rest;
Nor lamb shall from the flock be lost;
Nor nursling from the nest."—*Ruskin*.

QUESTIONS.

What is the motto of this lesson?
What is, "The group built for joy?"
What points of advantage do birds have over man?
Look up the temperature of men and birds.
What is it makes birds so attractive to man?
What are the pigeons' chief points of beauty?
Are birds remarkable for their pairing tendencies?
What families of birds are most distinguished for mating?
Does this lifelong fidelity denote a moral elevation?
Are pigeons changed in this respect by domestication?
Do pigeons require that their houses should be kept clean?
What color pleases them best?
Look up "Venice," "St. Mark," "campanile."
Commit "The Doves of Venice."
Where do the doves come from?

What is a "coigne of vantage."
What did St. Mark say about the birds?
What is his prayer?
Do such noble ideas help us to treat every living thing with more tender care?
Why do people cage birds?
Count up the neglects birds suffer from, those you know about, as well as those mentioned here, and see what you can do to make them fewer.
Are we excusable for forgetting dependent creatures?
If you have a caged bird make a careful study of its needs.
Commit Holmes' lines.
What use should we make of our superior intelligence and skill?
Look up Orpheus.
How may love and kindness help on the harmony of life?
Commit Ruskin's lines.

PART FOURTH.

In which the cruelty of much so-called pleasure-seeking is shown, the development afforded by true nature study is brought out, the importance of birds to agriculture is made plain, and a few great moral lessons are given by great men.

CHAPTER XL.
BIRDS AND AGRICULTURE.

"The poets are the truth tellers."

" 'Tis always morning somewhere, and above
The awakening continents, from shore to shore,
Somewhere the birds are singing evermore."—Longfellow.

"THE BIRDS OF KILLINGWORTH."—H. W. LONGFELLOW.

" The robin and the bluebird piping loud,
   Filled all the blossoming orchards with their glee;
The sparrows chirped as if they still were proud
   Their race in Holy Writ should mentioned be;
And hungry crows, assembled in a crowd,
   Clamored their piteous prayer incessantly,
Knowing who hears the ravens cry, and said:
' Give us, O Lord, this day our daily bread!'

" Thus came the jocund Spring in Killingworth,
   In fabulous days, some hundred years ago;
And thrifty farmers, as they tilled the earth,
   Heard with alarm the cawing of the crow,
That mingled with the universal mirth,
   Cassandra-like, prognosticating woe;
They shook their heads, and doomed with dreadful words
   To swift destruction the whole race of birds.

" And a town meeting was convened straightway
   To set a price upon the guilty heads

Of these marauders, who, in lieu of pay,
   Levied blackmail upon the garden beds
And cornfields, and beheld without dismay
   The awful scarecrow, with his fluttering shreds;
The skeleton that waited at their feast,
Whereby their sinful pleasure was increased.

* * * * * * * * * * *

" Rose the Preceptor,
   To speak out what was in him, clear and strong.

* * * * * * * * * * *

" Plato, anticipating the reviewers,
   From his Republic banished without pity
The poets; in this little town of yours,
   You put to death, by means of a Committee,
The ballad singers and the troubadours,
   The street musicians of the heavenly city.
The birds who make sweet music for us all
In our dark hour, as David did for Saul.

THEIR SONGS.

" The thrush that carols at the dawn of day
   From the green steeples of the piny wood;
The oriole in the elm; the noisy jay,
   Jargoning like a foreigner at his food;
The bluebird balanced on some topmost spray,
   Flooding with melody the neighborhood;
Linnet and meadow-lark, and all the throng
That dwell in nests, and have the gift of song.

" You slay them all! and wherefore? for the gain
   Of a scant handful more or less of wheat,

Or rye, or barley, or some other grain,
   Scratched up at random by industrious feet,
Searching for worm, or weevil after rain!
   Or a few cherries, that are not so sweet
As are the songs these uninvited guests
Sing at their feast with comfortable breasts.

" Do you ne'er think what wondrous beings these?
   Do you ne'er think who made them, and who taught
The dialect they speak, where melodies
   Alone are the interpreters of thought?
Whose household words are songs in many keys,
   Sweeter than instrument of man e'er caught!
Whose habitations in the treetops even
Are halfway houses on the road to heaven!

" Think every morning when the sun peeps through
   The dim, leaf-latticed windows of the grove,
How jubilant the happy birds renew
   Their old melodious madigrals of love!
And when you think of this, remember too
   'Tis always morning somewhere, and above
The awakening continents, from shore to shore,
Somewhere the birds are singing evermore.

THEIR SERVICE TO MAN.

" Think of your woods and orchards without birds!
   Of empty nests that cling to boughs and beams
As in an idiot's brain remembered words
   Hang empty 'mid the cobwebs of his dreams!
Will bleat of flocks or bellowing of herds
   Make up for the lost music, when your teams

Drag home the stingy harvest, and no more
The feathered gleaners follow to your door?

" What! would you rather rather see the incessant stir
    Of insects in the winrows of the hay,
And hear the locust and the grasshopper
    Their melancholy hurdy gurdies play?
Is this more pleasant to you than the whir
    Of meadow-lark, and her sweet roundelay,
Or twitter of little field-fares, as you take
Your nooning in the shade of bush and brake?

" You call them thieves and pillagers; but know
    They are the winged wardens of your farms,
Who from the cornfields drive the insidious foe,
    And from your harvest keep a hundred harms.
Even the blackest of them all, the crow,
    Renders good services as your man-at-arms,
Crushing the beetle in his coat-of-mail,
And crying havoc on the slug and snail.

THE CLAIMS OF GENTLENESS AND REVERENCE.

" How can I teach your children gentleness,
    And mercy to the weak, and reverence
For life, which, in its weakness or excess,
    Is still a gleam of God's omnipotence,
Or death, which, seeming darkness, is no less
    The self-same light, although averted hence,
When by your laws, your actions, and your speech,
You contradict the very things I teach.
    *   *   *   *   *   *   *

" The birds were doomed; and, as the record shows,
A bounty offered for the heads of crows.

* * * * * * *

THE RESULT OF THEIR DESTRUCTION.

" Devoured by worms, like Herod, was the town,
Because, like Herod, it had ruthlessly
Slaughtered the Innocents. From the trees spun down
The canker-worms upon the passers-by,
Upon each woman's bonnet, shawl and gown,
Who shook them off with just a little cry;
They were the terror of each favorite walk,
The endless theme of all the village talk.

" The farmers grew impatient, but a few
Confessed their error, and would not complain,
For after all, the best thing one can do
When it is raining, is to let it rain.
They then repealed the law, although they knew
It would not call the dead to life again;
As schoolboys, finding their mistake too late,
Draw a wet sponge across the accusing slate.

" That year in Killingworth, the autumn came
Without the light of his majestic look,
The wonder of the falling tongues of flame,
The illumined pages of his Doom's-Day book.
A few lost leaves blushed crimson with their shame,
And drowned themselves, despairing, in the brook,
While the wild wind went moaning everywhere,
Lamenting the dead children of the air!

THE RETURN OF THE BIRDS.

" For the next spring a stranger sight was seen,
  A sight that never yet by bard was sung,
  As great a wonder as it would have been
  If some dumb animal had found a tongue!
A wagon, overarched with evergreen,
  Upon whose boughs were wicker cages hung;
All full of singing birds, came down the street,
Filling the air with music wild and sweet.

" From all the country 'round, these birds were brought,
  By order of the town, with anxious quest,
And, loosened from their wicker prisons, sought
  In woods and fields the places they loved best.
Singing loud canticles, which many thought
  Were satires to the authorities addressed,
While others, listening in green lanes, averred
Such lovely music never had been heard! "

In speaking of the economic side of the question one ornithologist says that the bird population has been so reduced that the insects threaten us with a plague like that of the frogs in Egypt. The increase and ravages of the pests are appalling. One insect in one year may become the progenitor of six billion descendants. It is estimated that we already pay tithes to the insects, one-tenth of the agricultural products of the United States being destroyed by them every year. Michelet assures us that, if it were not for the birds, they would destroy every green thing, so that the earth would soon become uninhabitable.

It has been estimated that one pair of purple martins,

while feeding their young, destroy 2,000 insects in a day.

The larger number of our common birds live chiefly upon insects. Among these are fly catchers, warblers, woodpeckers, nuthatches, orioles, goatsuckers, humming birds, tanagers, waxwings, gnat catchers, kinglets, vireos, thrushes, wrens, titmice, cuckoos, swallows, shrikes, thrashers, creepers, and bluebirds.

Not only *these birds* are useful, but also some birds which are often considered injurious to agriculture, such as hawks, owls, crows, and jays. The Division of Economic Ornithology in the Department of Agriculture has had the accused birds on trial, and by careful examinations of stomach contents has proved that although they may now and then kill chickens, pull up the young corn, or rob a hen's nest, this is more than counterbalanced by the *good* they do in destroying grasshoppers, cutworms, and harmful insects, as well as field mice and other injurious animals.

The *Crow Bulletin*, published by the Department of Agriculture, proves that when corn is soaked in tar water before planting the crows will not molest it, and that the eggs and poultry which they eat amounts to only a fraction of one per cent. of their food, which is largely of grasshoppers and grubs.

The much accused cherry bird has rescued whole villages from the elmworm plague, and it is well argued that the birds have a right to a little fruit, merely as wages for their work—that only aggravated cases of perverted appetite can justify the shooting of birds. It is true that our

cows and horses consume our hay and grain, but we do not shoot them for that reason.

The Department of Agriculture suggests planting food for the birds that will draw them from the berry patches and orchards—Juneberry as early food; mulberry for a little later; wild cherry, planted along roads and fences, and elder and viburnum for hedges and shrubberies."— *Taken from a leaflet published by the Humane Education Committee of Providence, R. I.*

NOTE TO TEACHER.—I omit questions to this chapter because the poet's lesson is so admirably classified and clearly brought out by the sub-heads that no further words are needed to point the moral.

Be sure the lesson is thoroughly learned for this is of the greatest economic importance to our country.

The statistics in regard to insects and birds should be made a matter of memory.

CHAPTER XLI.
COST OF FEATHER ORNAMENTS.

Condensed from Leaflets published by the Humane Education Committee, Providence, R. I.

"Life and joy and song, depend upon it,
Are costly trimming for a woman's bonnet."
May Riley Smith.

" Are not two sparrows sold for a farthing, and one of them shall not fall to the ground without your Father."

"I don't want to make you uncomfortable, girls, but is it possible that it was one of you who had a bird's wing in her hat?"

" Just in front of my pew sits a maiden,
   A little brown wing in her hat,
With its touches of tropical azure,
   And sheen of the sun upon that.

" Through the bloom-colored pane shines a glory
   By which the vast shadows are stirred,
But I pine for the Spirit and splendor
   That painted the wing of the bird.

" The organ rolls down its great anthem,
   With the soul of a song it is blent,
But for me, I am sick for the singing
   Of one little song that is spent.

" The voice of the curate is gentle—
   'No sparrow shall fall to the ground,'
But the poor broken wing on the bonnet
   Is mocking the merciful sound."

Celia Thaxter says: "How refreshing is the sight of the birdless bonnet. The face beneath, no matter how plain it may be, seems to possess a gentle calm. She might have had birds, this girl, for they are cheap enough and plentiful enough, heaven knows; but she has them not, therefore she must wear within things infinitely precious, namely, good sense, good taste, good feeling."

In the report of the American Ornithologist Union, published in 1886, it was estimated that about five million birds were annually required to fill the demand for the ornamentation of the hats of American women. This slaughter is not confined to song birds alone—everything that wears feathers is in demand. The bulletin issued by the Union has the following: "The slaughter extends in greater or less degree throughout the country. The destruction of two thousand terns in a single season on Cape Cod, for exportation; a million rail and bobolinks, killed in a single month near Philadelphia, are facts that may well furnish food for reflection."

"The swamps and marshes of Florida are well known to have recently become depopulated of their egrets and herons, while the state at large has been for years a favorite slaughter ground of the milliner's emissaries."

One London dealer in birds received, when the fashion was at its height, a single assignment of thirty-two thousand dead humming birds; another received at one time thirty thousand aquatic birds, and three hundred thousand pairs of wings. Fully nine million birds have been killed to supply the London markets for a single season.

A great French authority, Michelet, has stated that there could be no vegetation, and therefore no life, if the birds were all destroyed."

Prof. Edward E. Fish, of Buffalo, in speaking of the great use of birds to man, says: "It is estimated that they save to agriculture alone, annually, over one hundred million dollars in the United States. In many sections insect life is still so abundant as to make human life almost unendurable. In other sections it is only kept in check by birds, and there is no place in which, were this check removed, it would not greatly hold the balance of power. The number of flies, mosquitos, gnats, and other small insects, destroyed in one day in a small area by warblers, swallows, and fly catchers alone, is beyond computation. From daylight till dark these birds wage incessant war on the enemies of man."

Birds preserve the balance of nature; they are the natural check upon insects, and the small injurious animals. But when man steps in to destroy them, the balance is disturbed and great losses result.

Many letters have been written by farmers and fruit growers in various parts of the country to the American Ornithologist's Union, complaining of the vast injury to agricultural interests resulting from the wholesale slaughter of birds. One writer from Michigan says, "The destruction of birds has been, and is, carried on here to such an extent that it is hardly possible to raise any kind of fruit, even the grapes, as well as the apples being too wormy to use." What a price for an ornament!

Margery Dean, in the *Boston Beacon*, says, "American girls, who have hearts so tender they could not step upon a worm or kill a butterfly, are guilty of a thoughtless cruelty, and make a barbarous industry profitable by following a fashion. It is thoughtless, for no girl in our land could deliberately allow creatures to be snared and slaughtered for the gratification of ornamenting her head for a few weeks."

Olive Thorne Miller asks, " How dare a girl thus endorse and tacitly approve cruelty and barbarity which she might know are a necessary part of this infamous trade?" Every woman who buys a bird this year insures the death of another next year.

The Snowy Heron

The egret plumes are not made artificially, as many suppose, but are the nuptial plumes of the white heron, donned only for the nesting season. The bird is ruthlessly shot while endeavoring to protect her young, her mother love thus becoming her snare. After the plume is torn out the dead body is thrown down in sight of the young ones, who are left to their miserable fate.

"WHO IS THE SEA BIRD'S FOE?"—RICHARD WILTON.

" By whom is nerved the sanguinary hand
   Which spreads a cloud of woe o'er cliff and water,

And drives these living sunbeams from our strand?
By thee, fair sister, wife, or gentle daughter,

" Who, to set off the glory of your hair,
For your brave hat demands the sea bird's glory,
Nor will one feather from your tresses spare
To put an end to all this tragic story.

" You are the sea bird's foe! You give the word!
Their snowy plumes to plunder, not to cherish.
That you may buy—the murderous guns are heard;
That you may dress—the lovely sea birds perish."

An American ornithologist says: " Plume hunters have destroyed about all the Florida rookeries. It is a burning shame, and it would make your heart ache to hear the wail of the starving young birds whose parents have been killed."

" What does it cost this garniture of death?
It costs the life which God alone can give;
It costs dull silence where was music's breath,
It costs dead joy, that foolish pride may live.
Ah, life and joy and song, depend upon it,
Are costly trimmings for a woman's bonnet!"

It seems as if the wails of these thousands upon thousands of starved and frozen fledglings would haunt every plume, so that no love of finery could tempt a tender heart to wear it. Think of it.

It is not only on account of the cruelty and suffering to the birds that we ought to do all that we can to stop their destruction. Many of the most beautiful and useful species of birds are becoming extinct; there will soon be no more of them, and we can hardly imagine how much of beauty and delight will be gone from the world with the songs of birds hushed. Truly, a garden without flowers, childhood without laughter, an orchard without blossoms, a sky without color, roses without perfume, are the analogies of a country without song birds. And the United States is going straight and swift into that desert condition.

*And this is not the worst of it. Boys with a birthright of sympathy and tenderness equal to St. Mark's, are being brutalized by this wicked traffic. For the sake of the money there is in it, they hide their eyes, close their ears and harden their hearts against the sufferings of the mothers and their nestlings. And who makes this sin easy to them? *Those who buy* the products of their cruelty?

There is much work to be done, but the first thing is for every woman and girl who wears a feather to take it off and put it in the fire. This may seem harsh, but what else can be done with it? Certainly it should not be given away to be used by another. You may say the bird is killed and the harm is done, and that you may as well enjoy it; but remember that so long as birds or feathers are worn, so long will it be the fashion to wear them, and there will be a demand for more. Even hen's feathers dyed, which so many think they can wear without doing harm, we beg of you to throw away also, for they keep up the fashion, and *that* is what needs to be changed. As soon as the magic word goes forth that feathers are no longer worn, then will milliners refuse to accept the supplies; then the wholesale murderers of birds will turn their attention to some more profitable way of raising money. The milliners will not be shortened in their art or in their sales. The leading milliner of Chadron, Nebraska, as a matter of principle, never deals in feathers. Her hats and bonnets are particularly tasteful and are in great demand. If customers must have feathers they are obliged to go elsewhere for them; but usually other ornaments are made so attractive as to satisfy the most exacting and unenlightened.*

Until recently it has been supposed that ostrich plumes could be taken from the birds without cruelty. But facts have come to light which prove that the plucking of these plumes causes great suffering to the ostrich, which has to be bound during the operation to prevent its struggles in self defense.

*When their plumes are allowed to drop as in their natural state, they are a thing of beauty to be legitimately appropriated by the finder or the buyer, but when, for greed or gain, cruel forcing is resorted to, all kindly hearts must set the fashion against wearing them. The world is wide and without the sacrifice of any life, is full enough of beauty to garnish the queens of all the earth, though every maiden should meet a King Cophetua. Indeed, the maiden whose heart is full of the kindness that casts out selfishness, whose spirit is too noble to take pleasure at the price of pain to even the humblest of life, whose mind is quick to see the truth, and whose iron will stands by it, whose hands are strong for deeds of love, and whose feet are swift on errands of mercy, that maiden is queen in her own right; God crowned; and there are none too high to do her reverence. Girls, strive after the adornments of *character*, not the least of which is mercy; beautify your *minds*, and *hearts*, with truth, and purity, and love, then shall our daughters be polished after the similitude of a palace and the graces of the lily and the rose shall be added unto them. Ugliness and cruelty will flee their presence together, and joy and beauty will reign with truth.*

The paragraphs enclosed in stars are by the author.

QUESTIONS.

What is the motto of this lesson?
Give the quotation about the sparrows.
What troubled the poet in church?
Commit the poem "A Wing in Church."
What was the scripture read?
Ought that to make a church-goer uneasy about wearing the wing of a bird that was killed for her adornment?
Who is Celia Thaxter?
What does she say about feathers on hats?
What is the American Ornithologists Union?
What does it say about the destruction of the birds?
How many rails and bobolinks were killed near Philadelphia?
How many hummingbirds were received by a London dealer in one consignment?
How many terns were killed on Cape Cod?
Are true egret plumes ever manufactured?
Look up the white heron and its nuptial plumes.
Who is the sea bird's foe, according to Richard Wilton?
What do farmers and fruit growers write in regard to the slaughter of birds?
Who is Michelet?

What does he say on this subject?
What does Edward Fish say?
What holds the balance of power against insects?
Who causes all this destruction of the birds?
Is this premeditated on the part of women and girls?
Who is Olive Thorne Miller?
What does she say?
What does an American ornithologist say of the devastations of the birds in Florida?
Why are the birds not taken when the nestlings would not be so cruelly cut off?
What is worse even than the destruction of so much happy life?
What harm comes to the boys from this business?
Will the noble man refuse to do bad work, even for large money?
Who was St. Mark, and what was his character?
What does true chivalry prompt?
What is to be done to stop the demand?
If the demand ceases, what of the supply?
What can one girl do?
Why give up wearing feathers of common fowls?
How may you help agriculture and horticulture by caring for the birds?
Is there enough beauty for adornment without killing anything?
Read Tennyson's poem of King Cophetua and the beggar maid.
How may girls be queens in their own right?
Will a truly noble spirit take pleasure at the price of pain?

CHAPTER XLII.
HUNTING.

"Only Life has any Message for Life."—W. D. Howells.

"Hast thou named all the birds without a gun?
Loved the wood-rose and left it on its stock?"
Emerson.

"THE BLOODLESS SPORTSMAN."—SAM WALTER FOSS.

I go a-gunning, but take no gun,
  I fish without a pole;
And I bag good game and catch such fish
  As suit a sportsman's soul.
For the choicest game that the forest holds,
  And the best fish of the brook
Are never brought down by a rifle shot,
  And never are caught with a hook.

I bob for fish by the forest brook,
  I hunt for game in the trees,
For bigger birds than wing the air
  Or fish that swim the seas.
A rodless Walton of the brooks,
  A bloodless sportsman, I—
I hunt for the thoughts that throng the woods,
  The dreams that haunt the sky.

The woods were made for the hunters of dreams,
  The brooks for the fishers of song;
To the hunters who hunt for the gunless game,
  The streams and the woods belong.

There are thoughts that moan from the soul of the pine,
    And thoughts in a flower bell curled;
And the thoughts that are blown with the scent of the fern,
    Are as new and as old as the world.

So, away, for the hunt in the fern-scented wood,
    Till the going down of the sun;
There is plenty of game still left in the woods
    For the hunter who has no gun.
So, away, for the fish by the moss-bordered brook
    That flows through the velvety sod;
There are plenty of fish yet left in the stream
    For the angler who has no rod.

A John Burroughs, peeping into a rock-founded Phœbe's nest with reverent eyes that note its pearl-like treasures without a touch, may come again and see the eager mouth-opening little brood. But if he lay so much as a finger on the moss and lichen-builded nest, it will be left cold and lifeless for his impertinence, and the miracle of voice and wings from out those tiny eggs will never be revealed to him.

How different from John Burroughs is the spirit that says: "This is a fine morning; let us go out and kill something!" and with gun and hound takes to nature's strongholds. Death, blighting, barren death, is all his finding. What a mistaken, misguided search for pleasure! It ends in wanton cruelty.

He who shoots a robin or a squirrel, cuts off the stream of joy that might have bubbled up to fill and overflow his empty cup.

Much so-called pleasure seeking, is but indulgence of

the lust to kill; a part of savagery that still clings to civilized man, and under this fair name of pleasure has been given sway unwittingly.

It is easy for us to understand General Sherman's statement, "War is a barbarism that cannot be civilized."

General Grant refused to review the armies of one of the great powers of Europe saying with high meaning: "I have had enough of war," and instinctively the love of the world's best, flowed out to him anew, because, rising above personal glory, he gave impulse to the truth that the prosperity and happiness of humanity, are marked by the presence of white-winged peace, and that the hope of the future is, that "Swords shall be beaten into plowshares and spears into pruning hooks. That nation shall not rise up against nation, neither shall they *learn* war any more."

The awful cruelties and irreparable losses of war are counted immeasurable by our wisest of men. What shall we think, then, when Jenkins Lloyd Jones tells us that "the brutalities of the pleasure-seeker are in the aggregate greater than the brutalities of the battlefield?" We must see there is truth in these words when we see that toy guns are put into the hands of children, so that killing becomes a part of their play, and cruelty becomes a part of their nature. But this is unconscious cruelty, as is much of so-called sporting. Again Jenkins Lloyd Jones says: "The word cruelty is allied to the word crude. It is related to ignorance. Stupidity is the mother of suffering, and thoughtlessness is the father of woe. Both are allied to selfishness. If he thought of the suffering of the turtle, of course the boy would not leave him on his back.

If he thought of the starving birdling in the nest, of course he would not kill the mother providence."

"The birds are the poet's own," says Burroughs.

A bird seems to be at the top of the scale, so vehement and intense is his life—large brain, large lung, hot, ecstatic, his frame charged with buoyancy and his heart with song.

Of course, if the woman had thought of all this she would never have wanted a bird cold and dead on her bonnet. The boy that goes hunting and fishing, like Thoreau, "without rod or gun," grows up to admire the hero of forbearance and say, with Emerson:

"Hast thou named all the birds without a gun,
Loved the wood-rose and left it on its stock?
O! Be my friend and teach me to be thine."

Such a boy would realize, like the Walden seer, that a field glass would bring the real bird nearer to him than any gun can.

The hardy pioneer who needs to hunt for food has almost, if not quite, passed away. Let him who thinks he hunts for food ask himself this question: Could more money be obtained by well directed labor elsewhere? Answer the question honestly. Self-deception is weak and wicked. If, on the average, a man can get more for his table from a day's work in the field, in the shop, behind the counter, or at the desk, then face the truth clearly, he hunts for sport! Sport? Why? Because he claims the creature's beauty? Its fullest beauty is its life, and he has put that past his knowing. To show his power? It is good to have a giant's strength, but it is tyrannous to use it like a giant. The strong should bear the burdens of the weak. To show his courage? The bravest are the tenderest. To satisfy the lust to kill? How the world recoils, yes, how all your better self turns with loathing from the Nero-page in history! It cannot be sport to kill. Cowper says: "I would not enter on my list of friends the man who needlessly sets foot upon a worm." The poets are the truth tellers. The world has applauded this broad humanity of Cowper's, but has been slow to perceive its application to hunting.

"Only life has any message for life," says W. D. Howells. Only life has interest for life. Only life gives joy to life. Learn this from the geologist that turns from the achean rock and gives his days and years to searching through all the earth's crust for the records of life. Learn it from the true naturalist, who with field glass and microscope loses count of time, watching the life of earth and air. Learn it from the poets who lead the world in ideal thought and feeling. Fear not to trust them.

Some say: "Our forefathers would have been overrun with the creatures of the wilderness, but for their guns and traps. Whatever may have been the necessities of the past, the need of self-defense cannot be urged in our land to-day, unless in a few instances where small animals, as rabbits in California, and squirrels in Eastern Washington, have become destructive to the fields. Prof. N. S. Shaler recommends national and international legislation for the establishment of wildernesses that may become sanctuaries of refuge, for all interesting forms of wild plant and animal life, that they may not become extinct through the destructiveness of man.

Some think it good cause to hunt for science. But hear what John Burroughs says in the *Century* of December, 1885, on this point: "Our birds are hunted and cut off, and all in the name of science; as if science had not long ago finished with these birds. She has weighed and measured and dissected and described them and their nests and eggs, and placed them in her cabinet, and the interest of science and humanity now is that this wholesale nest-robbing cease. * * *. The professional nest-robber and skin-collector should be put down."

Naturalists and lovers of birds understand well that the feathered tribes flock to a district where they are protected from shooting. It is a tribute to our humanity that as this has become more widely understood, cities of refuge for them have multiplied. Even migratory birds will return to places where they have enjoyed such protection.

One day, a West Washington robin, hard pressed by a sparrow-hawk, took refuge in the very arms of a mother, who was walking in the orchard with her baby. He clung trembling to her breast beside the little one, and knew that he was safe. The baby and the mother smiled their pledge of faith. Robin, doubting nothing, hopped on to an apple bough that almost touched them and trusted all in all to the three (the father was in the group). The sparrow-hawk recognizing the alliance wheeled away.

"Yea, the sparrow hath found an house and the swallow hath found a nest for her young, even thine altars, O Lord of Hosts."

What heart does not feel that it would have been a black deed to have killed that trusting bird, or even to have imprisoned it? Then can it be worthy of our better selves to repel the confidence of the happy dwellers in field, and wood, and mountain, by wanton waste of them? At the present day, there is little shooting even of geese and ducks, grouse and quail, or the fast disappearing deer and antelope that can bear the test of necessity for food. A few years ago I met a company of pleasure seekers of liberal means, who were returning from a hunt among the foothills of the Rockies. They struck a valley where evidently no shot had been fired before. The antelopes and the deer were almost as tame as sheep, and these men told with pride of the great numbers they shot down before the trusting creatures could understand who was the enemy, and fly. They did not want the meat, they did not even care to take the skins and horns from many of them, but only counted up their slain; for what? For glory? Oh, shame! The pain of this is not only that so much joyous life was wantonly wasted, but that the *finer sensibilities* of those men were so blunted. That there was so much unconscious savagery within them, well bred as they appeared to be.

This falls far below Cowper's standard, and the poets are the truth tellers. " Only life has any message for life."

If every gun were turned into a field-glass and microscope, an impulse would be given to civilization that would manifest itself everywhere in sweeter manners, purer laws. Arts and sciences would be advanced, but, most of all, family and social life would mount as on wings. Finer feelings would result in more careful consideration for others, and happiness would be multiplied, until the poet's dream would be realized. "And joy was duty, and love was law."

QUESTIONS.

Why are the poets especially the truth-tellers?
Commit Emerson's lines.
Look up Emerson.
Commit the "Bloodless Sportsman."
Find out what you can about Sam Walter Foss.
How does this poet go hunting and fishing?
What kind of game does he get?
How is the choicest game taken, if not with gun and rod?
What does he say of the size of his game, and how can you sustain the poet's claim?
What is meant by "A Bloodless Sportsman?"
To whom do the woods and streams belong, and why?
Look up John Burroughs. He has articles from time to time in the *Century* for the past five years.
What does the ordinary hunter say in spirit, if not in words?
What does he get?
Can pleasure-seeking that gives pain and fosters cruelty bring real pleasure?
Much that is called pleasure is, in reality, what?
Why has such cruelty held respected place so long?
What does General Sherman say about war?
Why did General Grant refuse to review the army?
Why did this high sentiment bring him so much love and honor?
How do the aggregate cruelties of war and so-called pleasure seeking, compare?
When does this training in pleasure cruelty begin?

If this were rightly understood as cruelty, would it go on?
How are cruelty and crude allied, and are related to what?
What of thoughtlessness and stupidity?
Would a boy be likely to hurt a turtle or kill a mother bird if he understood the cruelty of it?
Study and spread the truth of these great matters.
What is the position of the bird in the scale of life?
Do as many need to hunt for food to-day as in pioneer days?
Is the higher beauty of the game lost when it is killed?
Is hunting a fair way of showing power?
Is it a true test of courage?
Does any noble mind like the thought of hunting simply to kill?
Who was Nero and what is his place in history?
What does Cowper say and who was he?
Give Howell's words about life?
What is the thing of greatest interest in all the world?
Who teach us this important lesson?
What does your own heart teach you of it?
Does self defense require men to hunt to-day?
What does Prof. N. S. Shaler say about the need of protecting wild animals?
What does John Burroughs say about hunting for science?
Do birds understand when they are protected from shooting?
Do many people to-day forbid shooting upon their grounds?
What sagacity do migratory birds show?
Tell the story of the West Washington robin.

Would any high-minded person count it fair to have killed or imprisoned that bird?

Tell the story of the hunters among the Rocky Mountains.

What is the saddest part of this story?

What would result if guns gave place to field glasses and microscopes?

CHAPTER XLIII.
FIELD GLASS AND MICROSCOPE.

"Build thee more stately mansions, O my soul,
As the swift seasons roll!"—Holmes.

" O for boyhood's painless play!
Health that wakes in laughing day!
Health that mocks the doctor's rules!
Knowledge never learned of schools!

Of the wild bee's morning chase!
Of the wild flower's time and place!
How the tortoise bears his shell!
How the woodchuck digs his cell!
And the ground mole sinks his well!

How the robin feeds her young!
How the oriole's nest is hung!
Where the whitest lilies blow!
Where the freshest berries grow!
Where the ground nut trails its vine!
Where the wood grape's clusters shine!

Of the black wasp's cunning way!
Mason of his walls of clay!
And the architectural plans
Of gray hornet artisans!
*   *   *   *   *
Nature gives him all he asks,
Hand in hand with her he walks,
Face to face with her he talks."

From the " Barefoot Boy," by Whittier.

The boy that goes hunting without rod or gun gets the happy secrets of nature. What a divine light the poet sheds upon the work of those humble forms that ply their eco-

nomic and æsthetic arts close about us, under our feet and over our heads every day.

Knowledge of these things enriches the mind, broadens the soul and sweetens daily living. It may be had for the asking by every boy and girl, by every man and woman, as well as by the "Barefoot Boy." May be had for respectful asking, perhaps we should say, an asking like the Syro-phœnician woman's that was content with the crumbs from the children's table.

To such a one nature opens up her secret doors. Such a one may thread her enchanting labyrinths. But to him who knocks rudely the bolts are on, the shutters tight, the ways hedged up.

Dead matter has, for the most part, long been named and weighed and measured, but life in its myriad forms lies about us an unexplored world. A few of the great ones of earth have set foot upon it, gathered a few flowers and caught a few bird songs. Some have outlined it with an artist's hands that hint at its wonderful riches; but they are all too few, and their days are too short, for them to have caught sight and sound of a thousandth part of the beauty and music that fills this world. When every boy and girl, every man and woman, become intelligent, sympathetic obervers, like the " Barefoot Boy," we shall begin to know about it.

" How the robin feeds her young,
How the oriole's nest is hung,
Where the whitest lilies blow,
Where the freshest berries grow,"

Is "Nature Study," that every schoolboy and girl can take up, and have the lessons first hand, from the great wise mother herself. Begin in your own door yard, in your own meadows, orchard, wood, and mountain, and open the eyes of your soul, and you will come near to "nature's heart," and learn of her secrets as Hiawatha did:

" Then the little Hiawatha
Learned of every bird its language,
Learned their names and all their secrets,
How they built their nests in summer,
Where they hid themselves in winter,
Talked with them when'er he met them.
*   *   *   *   *   *

Of all beasts he learned the language,
Learned their names and all their secrets,
How the beavers built their lodges,
Where the squirrels hid their acorns,
How the reindeer ran so swiftly,
Why the rabbit was so timid,
Talked with them whene'er he met them,
Called them 'Hiawatha's brothers.'"
Longfellow.

Microscopes and field glasses are very cheap compared with guns, and as educational helps their value can hardly be estimated. In one catalogue of microscopes prices range from fifteen cents to forty-five dollars. Three dollars and a half will buy a very helpful student's instrument, and for twelve dollars one of great power may be secured, one that reveals undreamed-of life and beauty. A drop of water, a grain of pollen dust, a mesh of cobweb under this glass are fascinating and wonderful. With such aids cryptogamic botany becomes an easy and a most absorbing study. The tiny insect that is only a point to the naked eye, under the lens shows a marvelous perfection of bodily structure that fills us with admiration akin to awe. Microscopes are so arranged that any little creature may be imprisoned for study and then freed without harm.

A small field glass that considerably extends the view may be had for one dollar. Eighteen dollars will purchase one that covers a distance of eighteen miles. Think of it! With it you could take your stand upon some lofty point and have a bird's-eye view of a whole county. With this the shyness of bird and beast could not hinder your study of them and their habits. It would not be a half glimpse of them while they made a frightened run or flight for safety. You could study them at play, at work and at rest, with plenty of time to note every point. Soon you could tell—

"How the birds build nests in summer,
Where the squirrel hides its acorns,
Why the rabbit was so timid."

You may learn artisanship from a humming bird as she builds her nest. You may learn family courtesy from a flock of pheasants feeding in happy companionship upon the ground. You may learn self-sacrifice and joyful service from almost any mother in feathers or fur. Mother-love is a marvelous gift, vouchsafed, so far as we can tell, to all sentient life. At least no scientist can say: "Thus far, and no farther."

Under the able leadership of Superintendent Babcock, the schools of Oil City, Pennsylvania, pursue nature study in the fields and woods, seeking for heart culture as well as mind culture. At stated intervals observations are reported, and love and care for plant and animal life are made prominent in these recitations.

To see an exquisite fern growing is far more pleasure to these pupils than to pluck it and let it wither, and to carelessly step upon a daisy would be impossible to them. Like the poet, Lanier, they turn aside the branches of the noble forest tree "with reverent hand," and wounded birds and animals are nursed back to life and health in the various schoolrooms.

The effect of all this upon the character of these young

people is something marvelous. Gentle consideration of each other marks all their intercourse.

Make a careful study of the sympathetic relations of the animals that come under your observation. The field glass is an invaluable aid to this end. "The art of sympathy" is the most important lesson of the many lessons you have to learn. Indeed, it is the end for which most of your other lessons are set. Nature study that develops sympathy with every thing that feels, enriches and ennobles character.

John Burroughs reflects sunshine. People are made happier and better by his presence. Nature has been his great teacher.

"Hand in hand with her he walks,
Face to face with her he talks."

Life so splendid, so joyous, so beautiful, is ever to us an inscrutable mystery. Man cannot make it. He cannot restore it. But he may learn of it ever and ever more. Let us cherish it and study it with reverence, "Only *life* has any message *for* life."

In all, and through all, seek after character growth, realizing that God is over all; then,

" Through the deep caves of thought thou'lt hear a voice
    that sings:—
' Build thee more stately mansions, O my soul,
    As the swift seasons roll!
    Leave thy low-vaulted past!
Let each new temple, nobler than the last,
Shut thee from heaven within a dome more vast,

Till thou at length art free,
Leaving thine outgrown shell by life's unresting sea!'"
Holmes.

QUESTIONS.

What is the motto of this lesson?
What does it mean?
Commit Whittier's lines which teach us true nature study.
To whom does nature yield her secrets?
Commit the lines from Hiawatha.
What help is a microscope in nature study?
If you may not own a glass individually, get one for your schoolroom, and make original studies with it.

In the same way, get a good field glass, and let the school be divided into clubs that make excursions with it in turn.

What are some of the character lessons you may learn from the creatures of field and wood?

Look up the mother instinct among animals. See what wise men say about it, and observe it for yourself.

How is nature study carried on in the schools of Oil City, Pa.?
What effect does it have upon the pupils?
What is the most important lesson you have to learn?
Does the study of literature and history help to this end?
Does the observation of sentient nature help most of all?
If you destroy or lose a schoolmate's book, you replace it.
If you destroy a life you cannot replace it. Should this make us cherish it?
Commit closing lines from Holmes.

CHAPTER XLIV.
PEACE AND ARBITRATION.

"Their swords shall be beaten into plowshares and their spears into pruning hooks; nation shall not lift up sword against nation, neither shall they learn war any more."—*Isaiah, ii:4.*

" For lo, the day is hastening on,
By prophet-bards foretold,
When with the ever circling years
Comes round the age of gold;
When peace shall over all the earth
Her ancient splendor fling,
And the whole world give back the song
Which now the angels sing."—*Sears.*

Read the story of Florence Nightingale in the Crimean war. It is truth that is stranger than fiction. It is, indeed, the splendid epic of Mercy making her radiant way into the very storm center of the war cloud and lighting its Stygian darkness. She was marvelously fitted, both by endowment and education, for the work to which she was so singularly called. Her slight, girl-like figure embodied the deathless zeal, the unyielding fortitude, the matchless endurance, the dauntless courage, and the heroic daring that has glorified the soldier from Homeric days till now. But where others dared to slay, she dared to save. Where others had the courage to make a gaping wound, she had the courage to close and heal it. While others had the endurance to ply the deadly blade from rise to set of sun, and still on till the stars went down, she had endurance to stand beside the stricken ones and minister to them for "twice the space that measures day and night." What wonder that tears "washed off the stains of powder" at sight of her, and that soldiers, who could not touch her for the throng, kissed her shadow as it passed, and slept content.

So fearless was she in behalf of humanity that when the awful fruits of the battle, wounded and dying men by hundreds and hundreds, were brought into the hospital, and the commissariat could not open the storehouse for the all-important supplies, because he had no order from his superior officer, with the resolution of a great general in a crucial moment, she commanded, "Break down the doors." She was obeyed without pause or faltering, and the head of the army and the world, applauded and approved this war measure of the "chief lady."

Only a great soul could have done what she did, and only a civilized world could have received it as it was received.

At first, a few sneered at the spectacle of a woman in "such a field;" but at the last there were none too great to do her reverence. Potentates sued for her favor, and strong men were humble before her.

Gifts, and honors, and affection were lavished upon her on every side. No queen has ever received such homage. This was no passing whim of favoritism. It was a spontaneous recognition of a grand principle grandly exemplified in Florence Nightingale. It was an impulse against the barbarities of war; an impulse from the heart of humanity, which even now bears us on toward the realization of "peace on earth."

In the war of the rebellion, which followed hard upon

the Crimean war, the Sanitary Commission of the North, was the best organized force for the relief of suffering ever known up to that time. As the tender, skillful nurses came and went in holy service, they were often called "White Doves," and, in truth, they bore the olive branch.

In 1866 the Red Cross was organized and flung its banner to the breeze, that banner which has since been lifted on every battlefield and in almost every pest-smitten, famine-stricken, flood and fire-desolated district of Christendom, without regard to country or people. To this standard flock the brave and good of every land, taking for their motto: "A Citizen of the World, a Brother of Humanity." They war against wrong and suffering which are so blended as to show no dividing line. Civilized and semi-civilized governments give the Red Cross right of way. Its army fights on both sides, fights to save, while others slay. The German who wears the Red Cross binds up a Frenchman's wounds as skillfully and tenderly as if he were a Bavarian. Clara Barton, the American, was as ready to lead this steadily growing army of peace and mercy in Germany, as in her own home land, and in recognition of her service the first Emperor William bestowed upon her the "Iron Cross," that priceless badge of heroes, for the first and only time given to a woman.

After nearly forty years of such brave service, this same Clara Barton, in the ripeness of her seventy summers, goes into Turk-smitten Armenia, and, like Chevalier Bayard, without fear and without reproach, traverses that "death fattened field," facing and felling famine in hand to hand combat and providing a refuge for stricken ones and fugitives. The cruel Sultan dares not deny her passage, because in spite of jealousies and policies, the Powers will enforce these claims of mercy.

Can such work spread without a growing demand that war shall cease? Peace and Arbitration Commissions and Congresses are the only logical outcome.

The International Peace and Arbitration Congress held in Vienna in 1896, was attended by dignitaries, nobles, statesmen, officials, and thinkers from all lands; and it was the hopeful promise of the Arbitration Treaty soon to be signed by England and America, to be speedily followed by like treaties the world over. This is the progress demanded by the truest patriotism of the hour.

The peaceful settlement of differences between nations is as much better than a battle, as the peaceful settlement of differences between individuals is better than a duel. The Duel, indeed, dare not show its face in good society to-day: War has no better right there. All objections hold against one that hold against the other, and the objections are magnified with the increasing magnitude of the contending parties.

We laugh at the self-destroying narrowness of the man who prayed:

"Bless me and my wife,
My son John and his wife,
Us four and no more."

His motto was: "Look out for No. ONE."

Intelligent people understand that the prosperity of the individual increases in proportion to the prosperity of the community and the state. Some mistaken patriots insist upon this same stultifying prayer for the nation, yet nations are but collections of individuals. Selfishness always recoils upon itself.

The welfare of the race depends upon a practical recognition of this fundamental truth. Citizen of the world, brother of humanity, fast grows in meaning to the multitude, and therein is hope.

When the motto of Switzerland, "One for ALL and All for ONE," becomes the motto of every member of society and of the federation of the world, then, indeed, "shall swords be beaten into plowshares and spears into pruning hooks," and peace and plenty shall smile at every fireside.

Past revolutions and upheavals were inevitable, but the time is ripe for advance. Let schoolboys and girls learn that progress, peace and arbitration, are one, and let them spread the truth as they come into their full strength of citizenship, creating a tide of enthusiasm that shall bear us out into the twentieth century free from war and all its crushing, costly contingents. Economic art, science, ethics, poetry and song may run and not weary when "nation shall not lift up sword against nation, neither shall they LEARN war any more."

"THE DAWN OF PEACE."—RUSKIN.

Put off, put off your mail, O kings,
   And beat your brands to dust!
Your hands must learn a surer grasp,
   Your hearts a better trust.

O, bend aback the lance's point,
   And break the helmet bar;
A noise is in the morning wind,
   But not the note of war.

Upon the grassy mountain paths
The glittering hosts increase—
They come! They come! How fair their feet!
They come who publish peace.

And victory, fair victory,
Our enemies are ours!
For all the clouds are clasped in light
And all the earth with flowers.

Aye, still depressed and dim with dew;
But wait a little while,
And with the radiant, deathless rose
The wilderness shall smile.

And every tender, living thing
Shall feed by streams of rest;
Nor lamb shall from the flock be lost,
Nor nursling from the nest.

QUESTIONS AND SUGGESTIONS.

Commit the motto and the lines from Sears.

Thoroughly look up the peace and arbitration movement. If the books and papers at your command give scant information about it, write your favorite periodical asking it to publish a full history of the subject. In the same way reach out after the full story of Florence Nightingale and Clara Barton. After careful study, write essays on these three subjects.

Find out about Florence Nightingale's first patient.

Look up the Iron Cross.

Draw the Red Cross flag.

Look up the arbitration of the Alabama Claim.

Look up the organization and history of the Red Cross.

How has the work of Florence Nightingale, Clara Barton, and the Red Cross prepared the way for courts of arbitration?

Is war as indefensible between civilized countries as is dueling between civilized men?

What material, social, and moral benefits would follow the extinction of war?

Is the prosperity of the individual bound up in the prosperity of the community?

Is the prosperity of a nation bound up in the prosperity of surrounding nations? Is the cause of humanity above the cause of country?

On what principle do the Red Cross men and women work?

What is the motto of Switzerland?

In what way would that motto help society and help the world?

Commit Ruskin's poem.

NOTE.—Ten cents sent to the W. T. P. A., The Temple, Chicago, will give much helpful literature on this subject.

"THE VOICE OF THE DOVE."

Come, listen O Love to the voice of the dove
Come, hearken and him say,
There are many To-morrows my Love, my Love,
There is only one To-day.
And all day long you can hear him say,
This day in purple is rolled,

And the baby stars of the milkyway
They are cradled in cradles of gold.
Now what is the secret serene gray dove,
Of singing so sweetly alway?—
" There are many To-morrows, my Love, my Love,
There is only one To-day."—*Joaquin Miller.*

"The Thrush's Lesson."

A little brown bird sat on a tree
A-swinging and singing as glad as could be;
And shaking his tail and smoothing his dress,
And having such fun as you never could guess.

And when he had finished his gay little song,
He flew down in the street and went hopping along,
This way and that, with both little feet,
While his sharp little eyes looked for something to eat.

A little boy said to him: "Little bird, stop!
And tell me the reason you go with a hop.
Why don't you walk as boys do and men—
One foot at a time—like a duck or a hen?"

Then the little bird went with a hop, hop, hop,
And he laughed and he laughed as he never would stop.
And he said: " Little boy, there are some birds that talk,
And some birds that hop, and some birds that walk.

" Use your eyes, little boy, watch closely and see
What little birds hop with both feet, like me.
And what little birds walk like the duck and the hen?
And when you know that you'll know more than some men.

"The birds that scratch in the earth, little boy,
And the birds that wade in the water with joy,
Can walk one foot at a time, you see,
As you do, except when you hop like me.

" But most of the birds that can sing you a song
Are small, and their legs are not very strong;
Walking, wading, and scratching, they leave to the rest,
And hop, hop, hop, and fly with the best.

" I've many relations, each one of us sings;
We're called Warblers, and Perchers, and other sweet
   things.
Just keep your eyes open while out at your play,
You'll see what I've told you is true. Good day!"
Anonymous—Adapted for this Book.

"TO MY DOG BLANCO."—HOLLAND.

My dear, dumb friend, low, lying there,
　A willing vassal at my feet;
Glad partner of my home and fare,
　My shadow in the street.

I look into your great brown eyes,
　Where love and loyal homage shine,
And wonder where the difference lies
　Between your soul and mine.

I scan the whole broad earth around
　For that one heart, which, leal and true,
Bears friendship without end or bond
　And find the prize in you.

As patient under injury
As any Christian saint of old,
As gentle as a lamb with me;
But, with your brothers, bold!

O! Blanco, did I worship God
As truly as you worship me,
Or follow where my Master trod
With your humility.

Did I sit fondly at His feet
As you, dear Blanco, sit at mine;
And watch Him, with a love as sweet,
My life would be divine!

"THE LEGEND OF THE COYOTE."—JOAQUIN MILLER.

I heard a tale, long, long ago,
Where I had gone apart to pray
By Shasta's pyramid of snow,
That touches me unto this day.
I know the fashion is to say
An Arab tale, an Orient lay;
But when the grocer rings my gold
On counter, flung from greasy hold,
He cares not from Acadian vale
It comes, or savage mountain chime;—
But this the Shastan tale:

Once in the olden, golden days
When men and beasts companied, when
All went in peace about their ways
Nor God had hid his face from men

Because man slew his brother beast
To make his most unholy feast,
  A gray coyote, monkish cowled,
  Upraised his face and wailed and howled
The while he made his patient round;
For lo! the red men all lay dead,
  Stark frozen on the ground.

The very dogs had fled the storm,—
A mother with her long, strong hair
Bound tight about her baby's form,
  Lay frozen, all her body bare,
Her last shred held her babe in place;
Her last breath warmed her baby's face.
  Then, as the good monk laid the snow
  Above this mother loving so,
He heard God from the mount above
Speak through the clouds and loving say:
  " Yea, all is dead but Love."

" So take up Love and cherish her,
  And seek the white man with all speed,
And keep Love warm within thy fur;
  For oh, he needeth Love indeed.
Take all and give him freely, all
Of love you find, or great or small;
  For he is very poor in this,
  So poor he scarce knows what Love is."
The gray monk took Love in his paws
And sped, a ghostly streak of gray,
  To where the white man was.

But man uprose, enraged to see
  A gaunt wolf, track his new-hewn town.
He called his dogs, and angrily
  He brought his flashing rifle down.
Then God said: "On his hearthstone lay
The seed of Love, and come away;
  The seed of Love, 'tis needed so,
  And pray that it may grow and grow."
  And so the gray monk crept at night
And laid Love down, as God had said,
  A faint and feeble light.

So faint, indeed, the cold hearthstone
  It seemed would chill starved Love to death;
And so the monk gave all his own
  And crouched and fanned it with his breath
Until a red cock crowed for day.
Then God said: "Rise up—come away."
  The beast obeyed, but yet looked back
  All day along his lonely track;
  For he had left his all in all,
His own Love, for that famished Love
  Seemed so exceeding small.

And God said: "Look not back again."
  But ever, where a campfire burned,
And he beheld strong, burly men
  At meat, he sat him down and turned
His face to wail and wail and mourn
The Love laid on that cold hearthstone.
  Then God was angered, and God said:

"Be thou a beggar, then; thy head
Hath been a fool, but thy swift feet,
Because they bore sweet Love shall be
The fleetest of all fleet."
And ever still about the camp,
By chine or plain, in heat or hail,
A homeless, hungry, hounded tramp,
The gaunt coyote keeps his wail.
And ever as he wails he turns
His head, looks back and yearns and yearns
For lost Love, laid that wintry day
To warm a hearthstone far away.
Poor loveless, homeless beast! I keep
Your lost Love warm for you, and, too,
A cañon cool and deep.

Subjects for Essays.

1. Give your reasons why we should try to make animals happy, and show in what this would tend to our own happiness and the formation of good character.

2. State why parent birds and young birds should be protected; show their service to man and how difficult it would be for him to live without their help.

3. State the special claims that domestic animals have on man and the supplies they furnish him.

4. Picture our condition without horses, cows, or poultry.

5. Thoreau and his friends of lake and forest.

6. What influence has man had on the animals he has domesticated, and what influence have they had on him?

7. Mother love among animals.
8. The mechanical skill of animals, as birds in nest building, beavers in house building, carpenterbees in artizenship, ants in cunning workmanship, etc.
9. What may be seen with a microscope?
10. What may be seen with a field glass?

NOTE TO TEACHER.—The chapter, titles, and mottoes, all make admirable essay subjects. They are the more valuable because the pupils have direct study upon them. These essays can come in to great advantage in the language lessons from day to day.

HOW TO FORM A BAND OF MERCY.

[*From George T. Angell's Leaflet.*]

The opportunities of a teacher to educate in humanity are very great.

The children should sign the pledge, choose a name, and elect a president and secretary.

If thought best the teacher may be the president.

A time for exercises of a miscellaneous character, meant to be in part a recreation, is set apart by most schools. This time may occasionally be used for the Band of Mercy, and thus avoid hindrance to regular study. Reading lessons, etc., will give the interested teacher many opportunities for mercy teaching between the regular meetings.

The chilren should be encouraged to write occasionally compositions on the subject of kindness to animals and to human beings.

MERCY PLEDGE.

I will try to be kind to all living creatures,
- And try to protect them from cruel usage.

ORDER OF EXERCISES.

1. Sing Band of Mercy Song, and repeat pledge together.
2. Remarks by president and reading of report of last meeting by secretary.
3. Readings, recitations, "Memory Gems," anecdotes of good and noble deeds done to both human and dumb creatures, vocal and instrumental music.
4. Sing Band of Mercy song.
5. A brief address.
6. Members may tell what they or others have done to make human and dumb creatures happier and better.
7. Enrollment of new members.
8. Sing Band of Mercy song.

N. B. To any Band of Mercy numbering thirty and over that will send the name of Band with postoffice address of president and secretary to George T. Angell, 19 Milk Street, Boston, Mass., he will forward free of charge, "Our Dumb Animals," for one year; copy of Band of Mercy Songs;" "Twelve Lessons in Kindness to Animals;" "Eight Humane Leaflets;" and for the president an imitation gold badge.

"ONE BAND OF MERCY IN SAN FRANCISCO."

[*From the Call.*]

People in the Jefferson School district, which has its center near First and Tehama streets, are frequently heard to remark the change that has come over the spirit of the locality.

A few years ago a Chinaman was unsafe thereabout. If

he wasn't forced into unequal, hand-to-hand contest, he was pelted with stones and made to think that life in this country had more penalties than the annual poll tax. Woe to the stray dog or cat which ran into the territory of the young barbarians south of Market street. They were targets for slungshot and brickbats till they either succumbed to the assault or escaped under some friendly house.

When pugilism was popular in the West the urchins of Jefferson School had daily combats in back lots, and skinned faces, black eyes, and broken noses, as well as bruised hands and lame legs, were not rare things.

To-day the Jefferson School is one of the most orderly in all the city. And why? Because every school child down that way, as soon as he is old enough to write his name, is made a member of an army for the prevention of all the old evils, and no blue-frocked, brass-buttoned, guardian of the peace could have ever done a tithe of the good those children have accomplished.

For the last four years the principal of that school, Miss M. M. Murphy, has been organizing the pupils of all the various grades into Bands of Mercy. Although, at the first, the idea was combatted in the district, it has gradually increased in popularity until now every child seems proud of his enrollment. There are about three hundred and fifty members in the organization to-day, and each one takes the Band of Mercy pledge.

Every Friday afternoon, before Jefferson School has dismissed for the week, the different classes gather in the assembly room, each class being distinguished by a badge of a particular color—red, pink, white, purple, gold, or blue. In chorus they repeat their pledge, and then recite in unison this stanza from Coleridge:

"He prayeth best who loveth best
All things, both great and small,
For the dear God, who loveth us,
He made and loveth all."

* * * * *

There are songs, recitations and experiences from the boys and girls to warm the heart and quicken the finer sensibilities of even the hardened. A little colored boy often asks the principal if the Band may sing the "Mocking Bird." It is as good as listening to the average concert rendition to hear this from the Jefferson School. Bird." The chorus is really delightful, the girls singing on one side, while on the other side the boys whistle the air and trill. "Little Boy Blue" is also given in appreciable style. Then three hundred and fifty children march down the assembly hall in perfect order to the piano signals for the fire drill.

Miss Murphy says the children bring into her office kittens and dogs which have been saved from ill treatment.

So everybody is happier and safer in that district since that Band of Mercy came in.

How to Kill Humanely.

Small dogs, cats and other diminutive animals, particularly if sick or in any way disabled, are humanely destroyed by means of chloroform.

Place the animal, with a sponge saturated with from two to four tablespoonfuls of chloroform, in a small, close covered box, and allow it to go quietly to rest. A small, tin wash boiler with a close fitting cover, will answer. The amount of chloroform needed will depend on the size and vigor of the animal and the closeness of the box. Be sure that a sufficient quantity of the drug is used to insure death.

The young of cats and dogs, when but a few days or hours old, may be humanely destroyed by drowning, if properly executed. This can be best accomplished by placing them in a tight bag, containing a stone of sufficient weight to insure speedy sinking. Warm water should be used.

Fowls that are to be killed should be stunned by a quick blow on the head, and immediately sever the head from the body by a sharp hatchet.

All animals that are slaughtered for food, for health's sake, and for mercy's sake, should be stunned before being killed.

This work should be done by adults only. Children should by guarded most rigidly from sight and sound of it, and children need such protection more than while in their teens.

"AND A LITTLE CHILD SHALL LEAD THEM."

www.ingramcontent.com/pod-product-compliance
Lightning Source LLC
Chambersburg PA
CBHW031939230426
43672CB00010B/1979